THE BEST OF BEST NEW ZEALAND POEMS

THE BEST OF
BEST NEW ZEALAND
POEMS

Edited by
Bill Manhire
&
Damien Wilkins

VICTORIA UNIVERSITY PRESS

VICTORIA UNIVERSITY PRESS
Victoria University of Wellington
PO Box 600 Wellington
http://www.victoria.ac.nz/vup

Introduction and editorial material copyright
© Bill Manhire and Damien Wilkins 2011
Copyright in the poems and poets' notes
remains vested in the individual poets

First published 2011
Reprinted 2011

National Library of New Zealand Cataloguing-in-Publication Data

The best of best New Zealand poems / edited by Bill Manhire &
Damien Wilkins.
ISBN 978-0-86473-651-2
1. New Zealand poetry—21st century. I. Manhire, Bill, 1946-
II. Wilkins, Damien, 1963-
NZ821.308—dc 22

Printed by Printlink, Wellington

CONTENTS

Damien Wilkins
    Introduction   11

Bill Manhire
    The Next Thousand   25

The Best of Best New Zealand Poems

Fleur Adcock
    Having sex with the dead   31

Johanna Aitchison
    Miss Red in Japan   32

Michele Amas
    Daughter   33

Angela Andrews
    White Saris   37

Tusiata Avia
    Shower   38

Stu Bagby
    The boys   40

Hinemoana Baker
    methods of assessing the likely presence
    of a terrorist threat in a remote indigenous
    community   41

David Beach
    Parachute   43

Peter Bland
    X-Ray   44

Jenny Bornholdt
    Fitter Turner   45

Amy Brown
  The Propaganda Poster Girl   55

James Brown
  University Open Day   59

Alan Brunton
  Movie   10

Rachel Bush
  The Strong Mothers   64

Kate Camp
  Mute song   66

Alistair Te Ariki Campbell
  Tidal   68

Gordon Challis
  Walking an imaginary dog   69

Geoff Cochrane
  Seven Unposted Postcards to My Brother   70

Glenn Colquhoun
  To a woman who fainted recently at a
  poetry reading   73

Jennifer Compton
  The Threepenny Kowhai Stamp Brooch   75

Mary Cresswell
  Golden Weather (Cook Strait)   76

Allen Curnow
  When and Where   77

Lynn Davidson
  Before we all hung out in cafés   79

Fiona Farrell
  Our trip to Takaka   80

Cliff Fell
  Ophelia   82

Sia Figiel
    Songs of the fat brown woman   90

Joan Fleming
    Theory of light   94

Rhian Gallagher
    Burial   95

John Gallas
    the Mongolian Women's Orchestra   96

Paula Green
    Waitakere Rain   98

Bernadette Hall
    The History of Europe   99

Dinah Hawken
    365 x 30   100

Sam Hunt
    Lines for a New Year   101

Anna Jackson
    Spring   106

Lynn Jenner
    Women's Business   107

Andrew Johnston
    The Sunflower   108

Anne Kennedy
    Die die, live live   113

Michele Leggott
    nice feijoas   122

Graham Lindsay
    big bed   124

Anna Livesey
    Shoeman in Love   126

Cilla McQueen
  Ripples   127

Selina Tusitala Marsh
  Not Another Nafanua Poem   131

Karlo Mila
  Sacred Pulu   132

Stephanie de Montalk
  Hawkeye V4   134

Emma Neale
  Brooch   136

James Norcliffe
  yet another poem about a giraffe   137

Gregory O'Brien
  Where I Went   139

Peter Olds
  Disjointed on Wellington Railway Station   142

Bob Orr
  Eternity   144

Chris Orsman
  Making Waves   145

Vincent O'Sullivan
  The Child in the Gardens: Winter   148

Vivienne Plumb
  Goldfish   149

Chris Price
  Rose and fell   151

Kerrin P. Sharpe
  like rain the thunder   152

Marty Smith
  Hat   153

Elizabeth Smither
   Two security guards talking about Jupiter   154

C.K. Stead
   Without   155

Richard von Sturmer
   After Arp   157

Robert Sullivan
   After the UN Rapporteur Supported Maori
   Customary Rights   164

Brian Turner
   Fear   165

Tim Upperton
   The starlings   166

Louise Wallace
   The Poi Girls   167

Ian Wedde
   To Death   171

Sonja Yelich
   and-yellow   172

Ashleigh Young
   Certain Trees   173

Notes and Biographies   174
Copyright Acknowledgements   220

INTRODUCTION

Who can forget the recent pained tweet of my co-editor, Bill Manhire: 'the paper is dying!' He'd just opened his 1988 Faber hardback copy of Philip Larkin's *Collected Poems*. Okay, it's not quite as alarming as West Indian cricketer Chris Gayle from the World Cup: 'Bangladesh stoning our bus!!! Feeling glass break!!! This is ridiculous!!! Damn!!!' But still, book-owners will recognise Bill's dismay. Last month I discovered that my *Viking Portable Hardy* had become still more portable—it was being carried off by the bug that makes a queasy lace of pages. The evidence is mounting: things turn to dust.

Which does make this project a bit quaint. After all, the annual *Best New Zealand Poems* has been online for ten years and presumably will remain online until sea-levels wipe us out. If you wanted to, you could leave off reading this right now, tap whatever connected device you have at hand, and make your own Best Of, or several Best Ofs. In the contemporary mode of multiple paths and answer-back-the-teacher comments sections, fixing such a selection to an actual page looks decidedly retro. So why do it?

Because we do like books—those fading, failing homes in whose silent rooms the mites are, even as we write, eating our words. And because there are now 250 poems on the site. (Navigation—as if we were ships not readers—is getting trickier.) And because, as people who are paid to think about language, we were curious about what such a selection might look like, and what it might tell us about a decade we suspected—rightly, as it turns out—was full of life. And finally, let's face it, because it feels very nice to point and say, 'Look at this!' This book points at many marvellous things.

Based on the *Best American Poetry* series, Bill's original notion in 2001 was that an internet anthology would bypass the traditional obstacles of book publishing. In a letter to Creative New Zealand successfully seeking funding assistance to pay the poets, he wrote that the site would 'break through the distribution barrier which prevents New Zealand poetry from reaching an international audience'.

He built it but did they come?[1]

From its first year onwards, the site has done far better than expected. It now averages around 3000 page views per month, with just over a quarter of those coming from overseas.[2] In some ways, of course, it would be a little optimistic to consider the browsing of interested folk from around the globe, spending on average five minutes in the company of New Zealand poetry, 'an international audience'. After ten years of activity, there's not been a noticeable change in the fortunes of our poets. Are we eating at the top table now? (That the appearance of a Manhire poem in *The New Yorker* was a news item in the *Dominion Post* last year says something about our relationship to the traditional centres of literary power—though, to be fair, the provincial cringe was also understandable; the simple fact is, we don't get in *The New Yorker* that often.)

It is worth noting, however, that there was a place where our model made a traceable difference: Scotland. Robyn Marsack, a transplanted New Zealander and the Director of the Scottish Poetry Library, gratefully copied the format in establishing the *Best Scottish Poems* site in 2004. In the introduction, their first editor quoted the editor of the previous year's New Zealand anthology; while Robyn was to act as the editor of *BNZP 2009*. That's traffic with observable impact.

---

1   Bill wasn't a sole operator. Fiona Wright worked on the design and management of the website in the first years and then Clare Moleta has continued that support. And of course the task of selecting the poems has been done by a different editor each year.
2   The bulk of offshore visitors are from the US, Australia, and the UK, in that order.

Perhaps the real effects of the *BNZP* site will—and should—remain more furtive than any institutional reporting allows. The channels of change are seldom visible. Writers (and their audiences) develop from odd and accidental meetings as much as from planned rendezvous. It seems entirely possible that in some corner of Oklahoma or Ottawa or Ostend, there's a local poet in possession of our url who now believes that James Brown is the way of the future. And maybe she's right.

While we're doing the maths, I don't think it would surprise anyone who's been following New Zealand poetry to learn that women outnumber men in this book. Yet this fact—38 female poets to 27 male—is worth noting because it represents a considerable shift since the anthologies of the preceding decades. Jan Kemp was the only female poet among 18 blokes in Arthur Baysting's *The Young New Zealand Poets* (1973). (Interestingly six of those blokes have poems in our anthology; if this is a book of newcomers, it also shows a resilient core at the heart of our poetry.) Vincent O'Sullivan's influential *Oxford Anthology of Twentieth Century New Zealand Poetry*, in its second edition published in 1976 and reprinted in 1979, found two female poets (Janet Frame and Fleur Adcock) born after 1920, and 24 male poets. In the third edition (1987) there were 11 such women and 28 men. Fleur Adcock's 1982 *Oxford Book of Contemporary New Zealand Poetry* has only four women out of 21 poets. *The Penguin Book of New Zealand Verse* (edited by Ian Wedde and Harvey McQueen, 1985) had 19 women born post-1920, and 35 men.[3] By the time Oxford published *An Anthology of New Zealand Poetry in English* (edited by Jenny Bornholdt, Gregory O'Brien and Mark Williams, 1997), there were 24 female poets of that vintage and 49 men.

There's nothing self-congratulatory about the swing in our numbers; our selections reflect where the action is, rather than where any progressive ideals might position it.

3   Among the 19 women, there were six composers of waiata.

This anthology takes in many of the key figures to emerge in the last ten to twenty years, many of whom are women: Jenny Bornholdt (seven *BNZP* appearances), and five-timers Bernadette Hall, Michele Leggott and Anne Kennedy. (Of the major writers, perhaps only Dinah Hawken—a single showing in the debut edition—has somehow slipped off editors' radars.)

One final piece of accounting—and this will inflame some readers. By my estimate, more than 30 percent of the poets in this book have connections to either the International Institute of Modern Letters or Bill's old Original Composition class. What can we say? The even distribution of talent is a dream that only prize committees and funding bodies need suffer; the rest of us should order our worlds according to the evidence of our senses. Bottom-line: these are the poems that most excited us. These are the ones that most consistently brought pleasure. These are the ones.

Now there's usually an editorial disclaimer in these intros along the lines of feeling acute discomfort with the notion of 'best'. Chris Price, our most recent editor, found it 'absolutist' and 'Olympian'. Yes, this is true. Time's test is the only real one. And yet it's hard to resist running our own feeble ruler over proceedings. Philip Larkin—recall the dying pages—wrote about Thomas Hardy that in most of his poems 'there is a spinal cord of thought and each has a little tune of its own'. Ideas and music—that sounds like a decisive combination to me, and probably the sort of test these poems were passing when we read and re-read them for this book.

The other pain felt by the editor is caused by the limits imposed—a measly 25 poems from such wealth! (Only the aforementioned James Brown confessed an opposite struggle: he said he couldn't really find 25 that he wanted to call the best.) We had no such pains—the publisher asked us not to make the book too big, but apart from that, our only rule was we couldn't select more than one poem from each poet. Which did, in fact, cause us regret. Under a different rubric we might have included everything that appeared from Anne

Kennedy and Brian Turner and Jenny Bornholdt, and had a good fight over more from a few others too.

Of course we were also dealing only with what had been selected by the editors, and so some favourite poems of ours were missing. But already that sounds too niggardly; certain unimpeachably fine works were there, forever shining and ready to be picked, among them Allen Curnow's 'When and Where', Andrew Johnston's 'The Sunflower', Cliff Fell's 'Ophelia', Vincent O'Sullivan's 'The Child in the Gardens: Winter'.

We especially enjoyed finding the single knockout poem from writers who don't seem to belong anywhere much in this sort of accounting. Stu Bagby, Gordon Challis, Mary Cresswell, Rachel Bush, John Gallas, and Graham Lindsay all contribute alert, often funny, beguiling works. And it was hugely encouraging—and a testament to the editor's truffle-sniffing abilities—to be able to include a poem such as Vivienne Plumb's 'Goldfish'—an overpowering piece of writing which might have easily been overlooked since it appeared in a chapbook from the tiny independent Seraph Press.

BNZP has also been rather good in gathering up newer writers such as David Beach, Anna Jackson, Michele Amas, Amy Brown and Johanna Aitchison. And in this anthology there are poets of such newness that they're yet to publish a book: Joan Fleming, Marty Smith, Kerrin P. Sharpe and Ashleigh Young.

But how exactly did we make these calls? With, I fear, disappointing ease. Having both drawn up our own list of favourites, Bill and I met to compare notes. We probably agreed immediately on about 80 percent of the poems. Is that too much consensus? We read everything again before our next meeting, and settled very amicably, very satisfyingly, on the current contents.

Having landed the plum job of picking the best of the best poems, it was tempting to choose the best of the best introductions. The ten editors had lots of interesting things to say.

Iain Sharp, kicking things off, wrote that he didn't want
to suggest we were a nation of Billy Collins impersonators,
though he did offer that the 'unbuttoned, vernacular style
of writing suits the sort of country we are'. In the blogs that
concern themselves with NZ poetry—google 'Bill Manhire'
and 'evil' or 'Jenny Bornholdt' and 'chopped-up prose'—
Sharp's descriptions and no doubt his exemplars merely
confirm a feeling that a dominant mode of formlessness is
ruining us.

Elizabeth Smither, the following year, found the field
'as diverse and interesting as anywhere on earth', while
admitting that it was 'always easier (and safer) to choose
among the dead'.[4]

Robin Dudding, despite a near-lifetime of distinguished
editing—he gave Barry Crump his first publication—still
sounded surprised, overcome almost by the task: 'No "round
up the usual suspects" procedure can possibly suffice when
you discover that, just as every New Zealander thinks singing
for supper is a piece of cake, every second one writes poems
and manages to get them published.' Helped by his wife Lois,
he got over the hurdle of numbers, found joy even, though
Dudding's final judgement was sort of Crumpy: 'We write
pretty good poems in this country.'

Emma Neale, the 2004 editor, tried to unpack that
'good', writing about poems with 'a syntax and semantics
which mimic the mind's progress as it encounters experience,
struggles with it, or moves towards understanding. When I
read a fine poem, there is usually a sense of actively arriving
at layers of new knowledge, of discovering experience, or
even belief, *simultaneously* with the speaker or personality
in the poem.'

The next editor was also after the simultaneous when he
wrote that the poem 'is both the winding road and the wild
horse that gallops past us as we read, so that when we come

4   Our own RIP rule was that if the poet was active at the time of his/her
selection, we could consider it. This left no room for *BNZP* poets Robin
Hyde and James K. Baxter.

around the last bend, there it is, waiting for our shock of recognition'. Andrew Johnston, sensitised by his time living and writing in Paris and London, decided that, on the whole, New Zealand poetry, in its tolerance for variety, 'mostly avoids the kind of sectarianism that one sees elsewhere in the poetry world'.

Refining Iain Sharp's idea of the conversational manner, he wrote: 'More often than not, it seems to me that the best New Zealand poems derive considerable energy from the tension between heightened language and "unpoetic" subject.' So far so good. However, Johnston is enough of a formalist to see the dangers of the 'prosy, personal poem that purports to use language transparently'. Cue, one might think, a plea for another approach altogether. Not quite. Instead, Johnston's brief commentary on Brian Turner's poem brilliantly corrected the uninspired readings of what might be seen as 'straight' verse, suggesting that the so-called conversational mode was as strange, playful and complex as any other mode, and that such a poem's capacity to 'change language', as he writes, was unimpeded by any apparent plainness. Indeed, straightforwardness begins to figure as a kind of disguise.

If Robin Dudding found plenitude a problem, joint editors Anne Kennedy and Robert Sullivan, writing from Hawaii, discovered the opposite: 'We noticed that in 2006 there were far fewer books or poems in periodicals by Maori and Asian writers than others, per capita. Those writers—if indeed they exist—either were not sending their work out for publication or it was being rejected.' The notion of these writers not existing is a haunting one, if only because it seems sensible to assume poetry might be universally scattered rather than ethnically determined. (As teachers of creative writing we've also pondered this under-representation.)

Kennedy and Sullivan wondered if the solution was encouragement from the gatekeepers: publishers, editors, educators. They concluded by talking about the 'healthy oral culture in Maori' and the popularity of kapa haka— 'choreographed bodies of men and women moving to the charged language of a composer'—which, they argued, carries the same functions as poetry in other cultures. It's an enlivening thought but then again, choreographed bodies and composers sounds like ballet or dance or theatre or film even, and why would these other cultures then need written poetry as well?

The following year, Paula Green took up the call, writing of 'our hunger for Maori, Pacific Island, and Asian voices'. It's a topic awaiting further research. One thing we did note in making our selection was the strength of Pasifika women in *BNZP*: Tusiata Avia, Sia Figiel, Selina Tusitala Marsh, Karlo Mila. Here's a group, *pace* traditional cultural forms, who feel poetry is a potent expressive choice.

Green's editorial also picked up an image from a Charles Brasch poem—'Shadow of departure; distance looks our way'—and argued that distance was still the defining preoccupation in our poetry, though the 'archetypal New Zealand poem' was being resisted. One year later James Brown was hoping that poets would resist poetry itself: '. . . less isn't automatically best, but I will say that not everything is interesting or significant just because it is set down in lines that don't go all the way across the page.' Earnestness, too, caused him to go all Shakespearian: 'Forsooth, but we're a serious lot!' More on that later.

Like many of our editors, Brown had no trouble identifying what he called 'the usual frequencies of contemporary poetry . . . casual, personable . . . confessional, quietly insightful'. He was attracted to poems in voices outside these frequencies.

It was the frequencies of childhood that Robyn Marsack found herself tuned to in 2009. She felt that her own biography—leaving New Zealand as an adolescent—might have played into her selections but she also wondered, accurately I think, whether childhood was a particular strength of our literature. Still, writing from life was again something this editor felt compelled to warn against. For Marsack factual truth in poetry wasn't any sort of guarantee. Selecting Tim Upperton's 'The Starlings' (also in this anthology), she argued that the thing may or may not have happened to the poet, what mattered was 'his method of composition': 'the birds don't know "when to leave off", but the poet does.'

Chris Price amplified a note running through many of the introductions when she invoked the 'ghost anthologies' that move behind the one an editor settles on. Generously she supplied a number of links and titles to swell the enforced skinniness of the chosen few. Here Price wasn't simply covering her bases, she was expressing 'the possibly quixotic and old-fashioned hope that reading *books*, as well as individual poems, is one result these anthologies might achieve'. We think those italics are pointing in exactly the right direction.

Finally, something interests me in the commentary of a number of our guest editors, and that is the perceived earnestness of New Zealand poetry. James Brown's exasperation we've already noted; Chris Price mentions that she could have made a full selection of poems dealing with illness, especially cancer and dementia. (It reminds me of what people often say about our fiction, that it's dour and death-haunted.) Yet neither of these editors made that sort of selection—and nor have we. That is, there's obviously enough excellence outside the apparent default mode to make a case for a whole different set of qualities. And perhaps it's more the case that the *idea* of our grimness persists far beyond its actual presence in our best poetry.

If I were put against a wall and asked to make any sort of general observation about the poetry here, it would have something to do with, well, fun. Not a very high-minded concept, I know. A kind of buoyancy then. Or lightness, in the sense Italo Calvino asked for when he wrote that 'thoughtful lightness can make frivolity dull and heavy'. It's there obviously, wonderfully, in a poem like Rachel Bush's 'The Strong Mothers', with Mrs Chapman who 'heated records and shaped them into vases for presents'; it's there in the best baby-in-the bed poem ever written, Graham Lindsay's 'big bed': 'Her ring-finger hand covers one breast/

He sucks the other and fiddles/with my penis with his foot'; it's there in Anne Kennedy's rugby poem: 'Five-nil to *them*./ Fuck. And fuck/the conversion/too . . .'

These, you might argue, are comic poems and are just behaving as they should, and yet the same buoyancy animates several senior elegies.

When Allen Curnow writes '. . . Gently as I stroke/this child's head, I'm thinking, "Goodbye!"', and then goes on to rhyme 'season's crop' with 'wither and drop', the humour carries the weight—there is no weight.

You could say Sam Hunt is feeling sad in 'Lines for a New Year', but the sections open and close like strange and powerful riddles:

It's a love song
between a mother and son.

The son plays the drums
and wrote the song.

On the recording
mother sings the song

like mothers do. And the
son plays the drums

like a good boy. It's a
love song.

Instantly, I'd like to make that my blindfold test for New Zealand poetry: name the writer. And if Sam Hunt can manage, gloriously, not to sound especially like Sam Hunt, I reckon the gates are open.

You only need sample opening lines to catch similar acts of disorientation: 'I make telephone calls/to my bones, eat evenings' (Johanna Aitchison); 'All day today the ice melted./My name is Queen.' (Anna Jackson); 'The computer is dead; long live the computer' (Cilla McQueen); 'pity the

poor giraffe/lost on the frozen steppe' (James Norcliffe);
'I auditioned for the part. And this way/I came to dance'
(Gregory O'Brien); 'If it was tattooed in Maori there'd be an
indigenous Universe/in this curvy groove—but it's a problem
of bleeding translation' (Robert Sullivan'); 'Get off my back/
daughter' (Michele Amas); 'She emerged from the bamboo
forest/with a white, fleshy-petalled flower/and her gun.'
(Amy Brown).

Of course it's not all like this, and yet the headlong rush
into odd scenarios and askew voicings gives this anthology
much of its tone. Here are the first four lines of Joan Fleming's
'Theory of Light':

Andy goes craving all over the beach
With her red grip and her red grapple.

A red apple after dark isn't red,
It's a black apple.

Andy? Because that's the poet's friend's name? Or because it
makes a nice sound with apple? Andy also makes us think of
sandy. And where did all this excited utterance come from?
Did language itself cause the colours to pop as they do here?
Whatever work we care to engage in figuring out the meaning
of Fleming's beachcombing—and the poem as it progresses
is clearly not nonsense, not only sounds—it's that eruptive,
confident address which is grabbing.[5]

I find myself grabbed in this way a lot as I read these poems.
So there's confidence, yes, but also a feeling of agitation and
short-circuited stories. Facts come at us fast without obvious
illumination: 'Ernest Hemingway found rain to be made of
knowledge . . .' (Paula Green). The narratives crackle but
they often break down. There's immediacy but it can be
sourceless. And at the risk of pathologising the decade, it

5   In the interest of registering initial impact, my reading dispenses with
the poet's helpful note which goes a way towards explaining the occasion.
Collectively, the poets' notes form a remarkable resource.

looks also like a time of jitteriness, agitation. The boldness of
these poems is striking and often strikingly unresolved. Does
calm never come to our poor poets?[6]

In this context, I was struck by how a poet such as the
late Alan Brunton, who began publishing in the 1960s, and
was never 'New Zealandy' and always cosmopolitan, looks
utterly at home. This is how 'Movie' begins:

> I like dinner music.
> I like water in a clay jug.
> I like it when the water rains on me.

The vivid unattached declaration runs a strong line through
contemporary poetry, though Brunton was doing this
decades ago. Has he been generative then? My guess is that
few of the newer poets would have any clear sense of his
work. Indeed, having hung around with a number of them
in workshop rooms, I'm not convinced that the category of
'New Zealand poetry' is formative in ways witnessed by
preceding generations.

I was at university in the early 1980s and in NZ Lit, our
lecturer Father Frank McKay, James K. Baxter's biographer,
set a test based on the Oxford poetry anthology. To do well
in this test we basically had to learn the contents of the entire
book. Shamefully, I did this. I memorised the names of every
poet, their dates, and every opening line. And I want you to
know, dear reader, I forgot everything within a week. But
it also felt kind of good to have done it. And when I was
dreaming of becoming a writer, my model was a version
of that swotty kid instructed by a priest in the religion of
literature: I set about reading everything ever written by a
New Zealander. Kids these days . . . they don't know their
catechism.

---

6   Poems with low jittery ratings appear in this book by Dinah Hawken,
Stu Bagby, Bob Orr, Chris Orsman, Kerrin P. Sharpe.

In conclusion, here's a wild generalisation. When I read British and American poetry, I tend to have the feeling that the poet is always making a case for what he/she is doing to be considered poetry, i.e. a major art form. I don't know precisely how this manifests itself. A density perhaps, an upholstery in the language, a sense of occasion. What's shocking in New Zealand poetry—it shocks overseas readers—is, I think, the absence of this effort. All our efforts seem directed elsewhere. But where? Into pretending we're *not* writing poems. Jenny Bornholdt's great poem 'Fitter Turner' articulates this issue fiercely and movingly, but again and again our poets throw productive doubt on the whole enterprise. It's what makes the moment in James Brown's 'Open Day'—'We got trapped, but managed to get out/before the poetry started'—resound with national significance: we're *all* trying to get out before the poetry starts.

So if it's been ten years of feeling antsy, let's put scepticism in the mix too. And jokes. Always jokes. This is how Sia Figiel ends 'Songs of the fat brown woman':

The fat blue Pacific
The fat brown Earth
Thank you very much.

Because the poem pretends to be a song, the poet, pretending to be a singer, looks out into the crowd she pretends is there, and pretends to be grateful: 'Thank you very much.' Of course the real part of this transaction is our pleasure.

One oddity of the *Best New Zealand Poems* arrangement has been the agreed absence of a certain poet whose work and example have meant so much not only to many of the poets here but also to the reading public. Bill's scrupulous self-exile, perhaps necessary, is also a little undermining of the project's title—here's another of those moments when I wish he'd not had such a brilliant founding idea. (Remember, during this period *Lifted* and *The Victims of Lightning* were published.)

In consultation with Fergus Barrowman, the publisher, and a reluctant Bill, we've appended some Manhire to this introduction. 'The Next Thousand' was published in a special *Sunday Star-Times* supplement on 2 January 2000. This future-eating millennium work falls at the very start of our period and gives the act of wise prophecy the bad name it deserves: 'And goodbye to those long millennial lists,/all of the "this and that" and "this and this".'

Of course it's a poem which also takes great rolling pleasure in its list, piling on the predictions until somehow the incantatory power takes over and we end up feeling—as with all the best poems—that what's being said is indeed worth paying attention to, even at the very moment the poem itself seems to be telling us not to believe anyone or anything: 'Someone will want to be Moslem or Christian.'

The poem richly refuses us.

But then there's one thing left over: smuggled inside the self-cancelling ambivalent jokes and the infectious chanting, a bracingly straightforward article of faith, two lines short enough to tweet, sweet enough to sing, strong enough to set this book sailing off into a world the poem calls 'so safe, so dangerous':

There will be no more screens or screen-savers
but I believe there will still be pages.

Here then, for the moment, are some pages.

Damien Wilkins
March 2010

BILL MANHIRE

The Next Thousand

There'll be the same non-stop palaver
about who did or did not invent the pavlova.
Something like China will rise,
some sort of Empire fall—
not that we will much care, not being here at all.
Deep inside the organism there'll be the familiar orgasm.
So certainly something should happen.
Possibly arithmetic and frost
will tiptoe right to the edge of the forest;
the wild blue yonder may simply go west.

The lovetorn boy will descend
from topmast and tempest
and try to get something off his chest.
He'll stare into her eyes. Big skies.
Big skies. As for the puzzled past,
it will just get longer and longer
and generally there'll not be all that much left to squander;
though someone like Hillary
will probably climb something like Everest,
because something will probably be there.

But we won't care. Someone will work his way
up the touchline. Someone will be sighing and sighing.
Someone will soon give up trying.
Someone will make an improper suggestion.
Someone will stumble over the body in question.
Someone will want to be Moslem or Christian.
The one you love will be one in a million,
no one will visit the red pavilion;
but someone will care for the one who wept,
someone will note how the world is windswept.

There will be no more screens or screen-savers
but I believe there will still be pages.
March will give way to the furious winter's rages,
the dark night to the new day,
the schedule to the resumé. I'm sorry to say
things sometimes will and sometimes will not be
exactly what they used to be. Many words
will be thoroughly meaningless:
say goodbye to sound-bite and mini-series,
but not to miseries.

At the end of the day there'll be a pretty big ask
but not a big answer. Pines will march across
paddocks and pasture. Someone will take
someone else to task. And listen to this:
there'll be an amazing invention which might replace
     batteries.
Actually, no one will know what the fact of the matter is,
and hems will be down. Almost certainly.
The bad girl's parents will go to town.
There will be no cars but much traffic congestion.
There will still be press conferences. Next question?

Authors who stay in print will include Dickens and
     Nostradamus.
There'll be maybe a dozen more Dalai Lamas.
There'll be an amazing invention which could well replace
     pyjamas.
Someone will be out of his depth but go hell-for-leather.
Someone will be at the end of her tether.
There will be such astonishing light on the water.
The sheep will still go like lambs to the slaughter.
Some will hold back while others go racing ahead.
No one will remember our old blue shed.
Both of my children will be dead.

So goodbye to the one who knows no regrets,
who will surely be sorry; goodbye to the thundering lorry.
And goodbye to those long millennial lists,
all of the 'this and that' and 'this and this'.
And let us be glad that the big, repetitive world persists,
so safe, so dangerous . . . As for the lovers,
see how she saves him each time he rescues her,
see how they search the sky for news of weather:
such wide horizons, such amazing cloud . . .
the two coasts crushing the interior . . .

THE BEST OF
BEST NEW ZEALAND
POEMS

FLEUR ADCOCK

Having sex with the dead

How can it be reprehensible?
The looks on their dead faces, as they plunge
into you, your hand circling a column

of one-time flesh and pulsing blood that now
has long been ash and dispersed chemicals.
The half-glimpsed mirror over their shoulders.

This one on the floor of his sitting-room
unexpectedly, one far afternoon;
that one whose house you broke into, climbing

through his bathroom window after a row.
The one who called you a mermaid; the one
who was gay, really, but you both forgot.

They have all forgotten now: forgotten
you and their wives and the other mermaids
who slithered in their beds and took their breath.

Disentangle your fingers from their hair.
Let them float away, like Hylas after
the nymphs dragged him gurgling into the pool.

JOHANNA AITCHISON

Miss Red in Japan

I make telephone calls
to my bones, eat evenings
full of 12-year-old
video credits.

Crows snap black
on power lines, shine
beaks inside my leaf window.

My childhood home
is coffee cans, a frying pan
on the living room floor.

Mum is a Moritz stick.
The stove is a piece of dried seaweed.

At night I cover mother
in a yellow plastic hard hat.
'Goodnight dad,' I call out.

The road is dancing.
In the dark I salute
packets of HOPE
cigarettes inside
spacelight
roadside machines.

MICHELE AMAS

Daughter

The Steeple Chase

Get off my back
daughter
this is not dancing
you have sharpened your spurs.

Get off my back
you are giving me
the fingers
behind my head.

Get off my back
you have me pinned
against the ropes
the ref is on his tea break.

Get off my back
I am not carrying you
to my grave.

Get off my back
from up there you are
taller than me.

I will not race you
to the finish line
race you to freedom
I will not count down.

I am not your competitor
daughter
you signed me up

without my permission.
I am not your
leap frog.

Golden Delicious

She is sunny
she is sunny side up, my girl
running to meet me.

The other girls look lumpy
with their slumping shoulders
dyed hair and regrowth.
But my one is a beautiful apple
rolling down the drive
out past the school gates.

Blame

It is my fault
her toenails
her thighs
the hideous
hair on her arms.

My fault
she has too many books
it's making her schoolbag
fat.

Fat is my fault
I don't feed her
correctly, don't limit
her intake.

My fault
the failed marriage
I am simply

unlovable.
No money is my fault
what sort of grown-up
is an actress.

No brothers or sisters
my biggest fault
an unpardonable crime.

Babies

It's a feast or a famine
with sperm
wouldn't you say?
Some days they can lap at your feet
other days are shorter.

I see flakes of babies
on hands
on shirt fronts
on benches
on car back-seats

The old guy, toothless and cursing
wearing socks and jandals
is full of babies.

The college boy
has left babies
on his sheets this morning.

The Unborn Ones

The brothers and sisters
how stupid of them
to leave it up to me.

Stupid too
the German psychologist's
advice.

One child will now
bury her parents.

The brothers and sisters
salty baby mammals
have returned to the sea

turning into little grey whales.

Alliteration

Bullshit, she says
and *I better bloody not be.*
I watch her b's bounce off
the breakfast table,
stinging little orange and black
bumbles
stick to my hair.

The txt

*Mum come upstairz
my throats 2 sore
2 call out 2 u.*

In firemother red
I take the stairs
two at a time.

ANGELA ANDREWS

White Saris

for my son

What I knew of their house
was a blue garage door,
kicked-in at the middle.
A buckling dent.

You approach a scene like that
with caution. It takes time
to know whether to pause
or hurry, head down.

Their glowing white saris
on this grey marble day.
Outside the buckled
door, a station wagon, black.

I was thinking of you. How you
will find out. The black suit
you will wear. How the feel
of your best white shirt could hurt.

How silk might hang
in a cold wardrobe. I pushed
you through those people.
I pushed you along the road.

TUSIATA AVIA

Shower

to S.

That next morning as I stepped from the shower
I caught myself in the mirror, I was shocked
to see the marks like blackened flowers
fallen onto snow, fluttering down the backs of my thighs
like finding something huge and succulent and moving.
I looked closer between my thighs
and on the cheeks of my bottom
and found the purple blooms.

And right then, the way they say people on the verge of death
see their lives flash, I saw him behind me
I saw his hands twisted in black fistfuls, my scalp scorched
my throat curved up like an invitation glistening
to a blade and my mouth open wide
like the death cries of small gods.
I saw him grind me into the bed, the wall
because there was no space no space
between us, he was pushed so far
inside me the room had to give.
I saw his hands on my hips smash me into him
I saw his fingers dig into the flesh
of my ass-cheeks like you would dig
your way through wet sand
if you knew something was buried there—
treasure or a living child.

All I wanted was for him to break
me, split me in half
and then in half again
again and again
until my body was smashed out of existence

like the cliff that becomes
the sand that swims
inside the sea.

STU BAGBY

The boys

It's a funny old world
I tell the boys.
It seems that Bonnie Prince Charlie
was born in Rome.

'Och, *si*,' they nod, well,
they're Aberdeen Angus after all.
I call them boys
but strictly speaking they're steers,

Or *castrati* you could say,
though it's a word
that they might flinch at.
And to one who has a raw spot

I say, 'that is a graze,
and when you eat the grass,
that too is grazing.'
They mull this over

As we wander to the boundary fence
where Henare is finishing up.
He offers me some
of his trimmed-off branches.

I look to next year's firewood,
the boys make eyes at the foliage.
'Yes, thanks, Henare,' I say.
'*Si, grazie* Henare,' sing the boys. '*Grazie, ciao.*'

HINEMOANA BAKER

methods of assessing the likely presence of a terrorist threat in a remote indigenous community

Wake in the dark to the sound of a log
dropping to the ground in a distant timber yard
a train uncoupling in the village
the growl of something old
angry and tethered.

No. It's just your wife's gentle snore.
Don't allow the year to scare
the substance out of you—a woeful
fight between a toddler and a swarm of bees.
A predetermined sonata, but screamed.

Hide your Christmas funds in the empty
World War Two artillery shell.
When it matters most
have someone bend over your bed
to adjust the pillows, lifting and opening.

When she says Please don't leave me
Say No, it is you who is leaving me.
Choose the avocado and the yellow ballpoint
with the testament This pen was stolen
from Finn McCool's Irish Pub

712 Great South Road Manukau City.
For your final meal demand
beer and jaffa custard plus those twig-thin
chocolate spirals at two dollars ninety-five a dozen.
A fine writing implement melting between your fingers.

When someone says a pole without a flag
respond a woman in her pyjamas kneeling
on concrete. Post something
to PO Box 47 Taneatua
then wait for the small, brown flowers

to burst open. Listen to the
newspaper-reading in the next room
the crack of the page under your writing hand
something metal, unoiled
turning in the wind.

DAVID BEACH

Parachute

She would never have jumped alone and seeing
the world like an immense crevice she might
have abandoned the tandem jump if the
instructor hadn't had Greek god genes. He
smiled at her reassuringly, she nodded
and they were off, her fear turned to delight
with the motorcycle which gravity
had given them. She approved his delay
in pulling the cord. Then she realised he
was pulling the cord. She'd picked Icarus
instead of a god. 'Keep calm,' he yelled. Next,
more quietly, 'Sorry.' She scanned the ground for
haystacks piled ten high. She looked up and caught
a glimpse of the plane, a mocking feather.

PETER BLAND

X-Ray

It's difficult not to be curious
about this bone-man under the skin:
to think how he's carried me over the years
without malice or contempt. In return
I've fed and clothed him of course,
shared the same bed, been shaped by his will,
but even after a lifetime together
I can't say I know him, not for real . . .
apart, that is, from a broken wrist
when he once came peeping through.
And now there's this inner-map of his ills,
that ageing stoop, those honeycombed hips,
the thinning tail-end bits. But what
really appals is his Model-T look.
He's indistinguishable—except to the nurse—
from the millions like him who've come and gone
since one of us first stood up. Perhaps
it's time to applaud his ancestral support
and keep this negative by the bed. Even then
it'll be tough to view that crumbling master-plan
without a more personal sense of loss.

JENNY BORNHOLDT

Fitter Turner

It was a year when our bodies
surrendered—knees, backs, lungs—listen

to your shoulder, instructed my physiotherapist,
who was also studying English Literature

at university. *Wild nights/ Wild nights* she'd quote
from Emily Dickinson as she massaged my neck

which is still sometimes sore after one parachute jump
too many, twenty years ago. Risk was what I thought

was needed, and yes, risk was good, but I had
a tendency to overdo it. What wrecked

my neck this time was the garden. It also
took a toll on his lungs, which do not suffer pollen

gladly. The family cold, which hung around
for five weeks, showed no sign of departing,

on top of which I lost my voice, which caused
confusion at the doctors when I went after being

bitten by something in the garden. My arm
started to swell and the inflammation crept down

towards my elbow as I struggled to explain that it
wasn't my lack of voice I had come about.

Pulling my sleeve up seemed to work and the doctor
was very impressed, as was the medical student

who accompanied him. The doctor drew around the
    swelling—
a shape that by this time resembled a very large and
    interesting

potato—and said that if it got much bigger, or if I began to
    feel
unwell, I should come back up smartly. That night

the temperature plummeted. There was thunder
and lightning and hailstones the size of marbles.

We stayed inside for the next two days, with everybody
coughing and me unable to speak, resting my sore, red arm

while the new ceiling insulation watched over us.
At this point I remember someone commenting on

an earlier poem of mine, which resembles this one,
saying some people might think *it's not poetry*. Well . . .

There were the colds and the neck and the lungs and
the bite and then there was the hip, which is

connected to the knee, though not literally.
In between is the femur which my friend Marion

has broken. I have a Dutch hache in the oven (for the
    purposes
of this poem—if in fact it *is* a poem—I will call it

a casserole), which involves lemons and cloves and which
I have made twice successfully, once unsuccessfully,

before. (Currently I am going through a phase where
    nothing
I make tastes of anything. Or, everything I make

tastes of nothing. I hope the casserole doesn't fall into
this culinary hole.) Shortly after the neck came the knee,

which is where this poem really began. To explain . . .
something happened which made me want to add

to a poem I had thought was finished. I tried,
but I had been right in the first place—that poem had

somehow closed its doors, in the way poems do,
so I had to begin something new.

*

My knee I injured running up stairs at the National Library.
I knew this was not a good idea, but I was at work

on a poetry exhibition, excited, and full of a great sense
of urgency (poetry can do this to you). All day I ran

up and down the stairs in search of books and manuscripts.
When I woke the next morning my knee was sore

and I couldn't bend it very easily. I felt
an impending sense of doom. Since I was quite young

I have had *bad knees*—the right always worse
than the left. At 14, I had six weeks of plaster, then

an operation, then another six weeks of plaster, after which
my leg emerged, wasted and looking and feeling as if

it belonged to someone else. Around my knee
was an impressive scar shaped like a question

mark. After a lot of physio and lifting weights
made from my father's socks filled with sand

and draped over my ankle, my knee improved. It's years ago
now, and although it still troubles me sometimes, mostly

it's all right. I'm not meant to run or play sports—like
     tennis
or squash—which involve sudden changes of direction.

Poetry, being low impact, is fine. After the stairs,
I went to see the orthopaedic specialist who carved

the question mark on my knee. For the purposes of this
     poem
we'll call him *Chris*. (We might as well, because that's his
     name.)

We talked about joints and their weaknesses and that led us
to my father's rare, wonky ankle, which Chris told me

had been written about in a *British Medical Journal*. He
     promised
to find the article in the medical library and send it to me.

*

After my knee recovered and the poetry exhibition
opened, I began writing in my shed, which is up on the
     lawn

at the back of our house. Am I working hard? Yes, I am.
I've been writing and thinking and clearing a space

near the vegetable garden for another shed. This time
for the children. It's been good working to make room

for this shed, even though it's meant some mornings spent
with the shovel, instead of working on this poem. I've
     developed

a sore back, but nothing serious, just an ache. Like my sister
who wrote from London to say, among other things,

that she'd hurt hers again getting off her bike.
We're all getting older and sadder.

*

Clearing a space for the shed has meant packing
the vegetable garden into cardboard boxes and

moving it down the steps to outside the kitchen
door. Once the shed is built it can go back again

but I'm fearful of plants being trampled.
Shaun—our builder—is careful, but he thinks a lot

about surfing and sometimes doesn't watch
where he's putting his feet. Occasionally

he doesn't turn up, because the southerly has dropped
and the surf is good. I don't mind this. I like the fact

that he also has his mind on other things.
I knew he was all right when he walked past

the kitchen door one day and said *I smell soup—
have you got a bacon hock in that?*

*

Fitter Turner is an occupation I've been thinking about
lately. The words doing just that in my head. It's because of

my father's ankle. I think he could've done with someone
in that trade. Every day these words come to me, and then,

in the mail, comes the copy of the article about my father's
ankle, written when I was two. It's entitled

Congenital ball and socket ankle joint and talks of
a boy, aged five—my father—being admitted to hospital

with a disease of the cervical spine. This article recounts
how, later, my father, aged 21, presented with:

*a fracture of the tip
of the lateral malleolus
of the right ankle.
A small effusion was present
in the joint. A ball-and-socket
ankle joint was present,
and both tibia and fibula helped
to form the proximal articular
surface. The scaphoid was fused
to the talus and the cuboid
articulated with the 4th
metatarsal. The 5th metatarsal
was absent. Only two cuneiforms
were present. The second toe
had only two phalanges.
The right limb was almost
1 inch shorter than the left . . .
No abnormality was noted
in the skull, chest, abdomen,
pelvis, hands, knees
and renal tract.*

That came later.

The X-rays of my father's spine, ankle and foot
were the saddest things imaginable. I went outside

and moved some earth. For two days I did this,
until my back ached and my knees hurt so much

I couldn't do it any longer. I went back
to my shed and looked at the pictures again.

For an odd moment I imagined those bones of my father's
in the ground. But we didn't bury him. He burned

and became ash. When the red curtains in the crematorium
shushed closed to conceal his coffin, our son called out

hey!—startled by the trick of it all.   *Hey!*   it was what
we all wanted to say. The ash my father became

was shocking in its greyness and grittiness.
We scooped handfuls and scattered what he now was

on the ground. What more can you say about this?
Hey!

That it is not the worst thing that can happen?

*

In the middle of writing this poem I had a dream
I was wrestling with the ghost of Katherine

Mansfield. A friend suggested it was a poem
I was struggling with. Yes. *This one.* Which I know

seems very plain and straightforward and
conversational, but it's taken a lot to get it

this way. Today I will take the casserole to Marion
who can now manage on one crutch, which is good,

because her husband (who coached the rowing crew
I was coxswain for, after being told I shouldn't row

on account of my knees) is about to have a knee
replacement and she needs to be able to get around.

Tomorrow I fly to Nelson. I don't like flying,
but I will grit my teeth and get on the plane.

Last time I flew on a small plane,
the pilot said before take-off *Lifejackets*

*are under your seats. If anything happens, put them
on. Don't wait for me to tell you what to do*

because I'll be out of here. In Nelson I will be met
by a woman who describes herself as having

'the ponytail of indifference'. I look forward
to this. She will drive me to the Rosy Glow

Chocolate Shop, above which I will stay. I will
lie down on the comfortable bed, then I will

get up and go and read some poems. Later
I will go to a Haydn Mass with the woman

with the ponytail, who will sleep a beautiful,
attentive sleep through the third and fourth movements.

Next morning I will buy some chocolates from
Rosy Glow and go to the airport in a taxi driven by

'Dickie' who has woken up deaf in one ear.
Maybe the doctor? I will yell. *Twelve thirty*

he'll reply, then pass me a mint. I'll head home
on a plane flown by a pilot who doesn't know

his left from his right, and from the air I'll see
our house and my shed and the frame

of the new shed taking shape by the vegetable garden.
The weather will be beautiful and I'll remember

that today is the day a friend may learn that his life
will be shorter than he would ever wish. Two friends

will tell me their mothers are dying. My son
will collect a cricket bat in the face and his eye

will turn the colours of evening. To pass the time
at the hospital he will ask me to list the things

that never end: space, time, the universe,
dogs barking at the mailman, numbers, weather,

fear, love, kindness, television, Haydn's mass . . .
Then a doctor will come, and because we live

in a very small pocket in the great big frock
of the world, he will be the chairman of my son's

school board of trustees. He is a kind man and a good
doctor, and he will patch up my son's cheek and we'll

head home. On the way I will think about the poetry
reading and how, beforehand, I met a man who makes

furniture, but originally trained as a fitter and
turner. *Do I know what that is?* And how,

in the middle of the reading, I glanced down at my book
and a tiny green praying mantis

scrambled bright and awkward over the page.
I will tell my son about this. He will suggest

I might have carried the insect in my bag, all the way
from Wellington, all the way from the vegetable garden

in boxes, and I'll say *yes, I might have*. And we'll agree
that wherever it came from, it seems like a good sign.

And we'll drive home—his eye matching sky—which is
an easy rhyme, but pleasing, to me, nevertheless.

AMY BROWN

The Propaganda Poster Girl

I

She has emerged from the bamboo forest
with a white, fleshy-petalled flower

and her gun.
Save the country,

save the youth
she is supposed to say

because she is young and solid looking.
She looks out at her admirers

and critics, distracting them with her stare,
the clever pattern in her headscarf,

that poorly foreshortened thumb
and dark pink fist.

She is flat and smooth.
Foreigners smile at her,

wanting to look good.

II

Duong Ngoc Canh painted me
in 1945. Then someone else
carved my image in wood
and multiplied me.

I was all over the city,
flapping against plane trees
and rolling down the street
with other rubbish.

Not quite immortal or free from aging
I was still luckier than most
for I had hundreds and hundreds
of lives.

The way you shed eyelashes and skin,   `
I let my replicas go painlessly.
Somewhere in the city, a printing press
was constantly replacing

what I'd lost.

III

He admires her elegance,
that crisp feline stare,
her constantly changing surveillance

over the tiny gallery's entrance.
It's not his first visit here.
But still, he admires the elegance

of his situation, the quiet insistence
of her gun (the same black as her hair).
Her constantly changing surveillance,

warm then cold; if only he could rinse
himself in her stare.
He admires her elegance.

To him, the print's
worth more than American dollars just for
that constantly changing surveillance.

They leave the shop together, an odd pair—
she tucked under his arm with a look of despair.
He, admiring the elegance
of her constantly changing surveillance.

IV

People like to be looked at,
especially by beautiful eyes.
But only up to a point.
Eventually they
are no longer open
to critique, which is why

you should stare secretly. Why
believe me? I have experience at
observing. My eyes are always open.
At times I hate my wide painted eyes,
though I'm becoming wiser. They,
I now realise, give my life a point.

That gun slung over my shoulder, the point
of the barrel behind my headscarf. Why,
that's no weapon. My hands are frozen. They
could never pull a trigger. Now, look at
the magnolia between my fingers, my eyes
can't see it. They only stare out, wide open—

immutably, frustratingly open.
An artist carved them with the point
of his tiny print knife, thinking, 'Eyes
as beautiful as a cat's. Why
not?' Carefully prepared, I ended up at
the gallery, alone with my sight. They,

the art dealer and her daughter, sold me. They
made twenty US dollars from a man with an open-
mouthed smile. He seemed to stare at

everything. Cycling us through Hanoi, he pointed
out the lake, as if he knew I could see. Why
he understands me I can't say. But his eyes

are so glad—pale-lashed, green eyes—
that I forget to question his awareness. They
flatter me, sympathise, know why
it's hard to be always open
to malice, accepting it wide-eyed; that's my point.
I am obliged to look out at

my viewers, constantly, eyes open
like a clear conscience. The man realises this point;
he needs to look at me, and to be looked at.

JAMES BROWN

University Open Day

English was the uncoolest: awkward people
reading Shakespeare in a room.
We got trapped, but managed to get out
before the poetry started.

Food Tech was okay, with fresh bread
dyed to look mouldy, and bright blue juice
that it was easy to guess was lemon.
You could buy cans of air, too.

There was a long queue at Chemistry
because you got to make potions.
One of the white-coats
came rushing out in a real lather.

Psychology had us reading
a short paragraph describing 'Mr Smith',
then answering questions about his
personality. Opinions divided neatly.

The trick turned out to be a single word.
Some paragraphs described Mr Smith
as 'warm', others as 'cold'.
The psychologists beamed cleverly.

'Applied commonsense,' snorted a man
wearing a *Microbiologists
          are Little Buggers* T-shirt.
Outside, padded eggs were being dropped

from a rooftop. Engineering.
People kept saying Vet was best.
It had the cow with the glass panel.
Actually, the panel wasn't that interesting,

sort of dark and red. The cow
was eating hay in a small concrete room.
Mostly it just ate, but now and then
it would look sadly round at everyone,

and that's when I got to thinking
about Philosophy.
The department wasn't easy to find.
It turned out to be a single office

down a badly lit corridor.
A faded note on the door said
'Back in 10'. And so
my education began.

ALAN BRUNTON

Movie

1
I like dinner music.
I like water in a clay jug.
I like it when the water rains on me.

2
I was just a tourist in those mountains. I drove wildly down
steep slopes through gorges and cascades. After the brutal
descent, I arrived at a belvedere with a breath-taking view.

3
I will tell you something: In 1897, three fragments of a
broken jug were discovered in Egypt. They were 3000 years
old. Poems were painted on the fragments. One of them is
        the poet smells his lover's shirt . . .
In 1951, French Egyptologists found twenty-eight more
pieces of the same jug and the rest of the poem was restored
        that sniff of sweetness instantly
        transports him to the South Seas

4
O Rio dos Poetas

I met a sage in a state of bliss
who subsisted on a glass of milk each day.
Below him stretched a great emptiness
carved out of existence, the head-waters
of the Mondego River.
A short distance away was
the birthplace of the 'discoverer' of Brazil.

5
My father died in December.
With my brothers I carried him
to the low house reserved
for dead soldiers.
When it was my turn to speak
I recalled driving though green paddocks
in his Chevrolet,
the road driving into my eyes.
It was the first day of the holidays.
We got lost in the traffic
and separated from the cortege
so we stopped for sandwiches and beer
and played billiards in a club.
A band was set up to play
but after a dispute with the management
they took their gear away.
I hope I never
I hope I never
see that part of Auckland again.

6
Language is my neighbourhood.
I live in Alphabet City.
The people who live here open their hearts to the sun.

Today was the birthday of Louis Braille, the inventor of a
reading system for the blind,
the day the sputnik fell back to Earth.

My horoscope says:
'Writing frequently will help you sustain a relationship with
someone at a distance.'

7

At night I watch the moon and imagine exciting places over
the horizon. Only a fool does not see that the vast industrial
economies are temporary. I say too much. My throat is
infected with words. At the country hospital, I am treated
by a beautiful doctor.

That evening we drink wine from the valley on the balcony
of the hotel. Look, she says, the moon is moving into the
distance, three centimetres each year, which is the speed
at which fingernails grow! We sing revolutionary songs
until all hours, drinking to friendship between our two
countries.

In her language, the word for 'Sunday' is 'resurrection'. I
leave the following morning.

8

This existence is not the original.
	Like love itself,
the universe is mostly smoke and mirrors,
	I am I,
the beginning of illusion.
	You are you,
the centre of confusion.
	I write to you alone at night,
speaking into the silence.

RACHEL BUSH

The Strong Mothers

Where are the mothers who held power
and children, preserved peaches
in season, understood about
greens and two classes of protein
who drove cars or did not have a licence
who laughed, raged and were there?
Take Mrs Russell who rode her irate bike,
an upright fly that buzzed
with a small engine on its back wheel
up South Road past the school football field
on her way to the hospital. Consider
the other Mrs Russell, drama judge, teacher of
speech and elocution in a small front room,
part-time reporter on the *Hawera Star.*
And Mrs Ellingham who had an MA in French,
ah, the university. Or Mrs Smith, one knee stiff
with TB, her tennis parties on Saturdays, adults
on banks and we smoked their cigarettes in the bamboo.
Her legs shone, their skin in diamonds like a lizard's.
Then Mrs Chapman who sang in the church choir,
formed brooches from fresh white bread,
made you look for a needle till you found it,
heated records and shaped them into vases for presents
who did a spring display in the window of Gamages Hats.

They have left the vowels uncorrected, the stories
    unproofed.
They have rested their bicycles inside their garages,
looked up the last word, la dernière mot, in Harraps
    Dictionary,
let needles lie in the narrow dust between verandah boards.
They have tested the last jam on a saucer by a window
comforted the last crying child they will ever see,

and left. How we miss them and their great strength.
Wait for us, we say, wait for me.
And they will.

KATE CAMP

Mute song

i

The first time I saw you
I don't know which I loved more
you with your tranquil neck
calmly transporting yourself through the world
or the one who followed you everywhere
trolling the dark waters like a hook.

ii

The strange thing was that
as each other's opposite and negative
we were even visible
I with my tatty winter coat
smelling of reeds
you consisting entirely of surfaces
or should I say one fabulously curved surface
smooth and white as an egg.

iii

I have no idea what you saw when you looked at me
a shadow dully pursued by the shape that cast it
a placeholder reserving a space from nonexistence.
Perhaps you saw God's fearsome ability
to be absent, his morosely taken option
to hoard his riches in another universe.
In anyone else, such a thought would be absurd.
In your case, it was luminous and adorable
shining in the dark location known as me.

iv

It was inevitable I would follow you
the sound of laughing that came
though you never laughed
the sweet nonsensical conversations
in which you remained impassively silent
the pointless journeys you took
your eyes perfectly round.
My desire was the desire to be superlative
I, who had spent years in domestic craft
became selfishly single-minded as an artist
inflicting your beauty on myself
like some ecstatic adolescent
cutting her arm with a pocket knife.

v

At night I would disappear.
You and the moon would glow.
I hated to think of the dark
covering you over like a mouth.

ALISTAIR TE ARIKI CAMPBELL

Tidal
For Meg: 1937–2007

I wrote this poem for you
Out of tidal wrack.
I spoke my lines to the wind,
And the wind blew them back.

This is my last poem.
It's out there on the beach
For the first high tide to turn,
And float it out of reach.

1 June 2007

GORDON CHALLIS

Walking an imaginary dog

You have to do this where I live—
the caravan park does not allow real ones.
Every morning
I slip out before too many people are around
dragging the dog at first
finding any spare power points
available to charge him up;
those with caravans already there
he pisses on
discharging an electrolytic urine
which strips the paint.
Then we try
outside the park: the sandflats of the creek,
the oyster-bladed rocks, the mangroves'
many attempts to start out again for heaven.

He sniffs heaven
in onion smells before the steak goes on
and makes no judgement whether breakfast
is the right time.

I go behind him holding the leash
gently though not letting him
surge too far foraging ahead
not too far down my road.
To passers-by I would appear
a blind man trusting my hand
to scan for obstacles or
reaching out to touch the small face of a child.

GEOFF COCHRANE

Seven Unposted Postcards to My Brother

1.

Turn fifty, Steve,
and it all hoves into view!
And why when one gets old
must one look so hideous?
While lingering of course
in some grotty council flat
with basketball at midnight in the halls?

Better by far
to live life backwards
from the grave to the cradle.

2.

Tamar Street and Kneebone's butchery,
saveloys and shillings for the gas.

I had the top bunk.
A cheapish crucifix
with a skinny, tinny Christ
had been fixed to the wall above my pillow;
up there with me too
were a Mitchell bomber, *The Satan Bug*
and a book on conjuring.

I'd never be so well equipped again.

3.

Landing now and then a mucoid sprat,
we'd fish a brown lagoon
in which had somehow sunk
a girthsome boiler fouled by mustard rusts.

Or I'd take you to the pictures.

4.

Sculpted curtains stained
by lights of lime or rose.

Ben-Hur and *Billy Budd* and *Bullitt*.

5.

ART CHANGES NOTHING

Isn't that what we were taught?
Isn't that what we inferred
we should believe?

6.

You sported as a kid
a woggy mop of hair.

In time, you'd find a purchase on the world
in the teachings of Bahá'u'lláh.
Become a subtle painter,
a provident and gentle patriarch.

7.

As altar boys, we had our separate gigs:
you did the church, and I did the convent.

Tight-lipped as spies,
we'd pass one another at the gate,
our missions shadily divergent.

GLENN COLQUHOUN

To a woman who fainted recently at a poetry reading

A blood pressure of ninety millimetres of mercury is normally required to adequately perfuse the central nervous system. If the head is lowered, however, the pressure needed to maintain consciousness is considerably lower. Of course if one has severed a major artery or torn it lengthwise like a weak seam in the lining of a jacket then poetry should not be blamed and, in fact, may become entirely appropriate.

It is wise to consider hypoglycaemia as a contributing factor. I have heard that a barley sugar placed per rectum in obtunded patients with a precipitously low serum glucose may at times mean the difference between them dying and never eating barley sugar again.

Simple dehydration, overheating or a sudden shock can also be associated with fainting. For this last reason poetry should not be left lying around especially if it is graphic in nature, with swear words in it like 'bugger' or 'bastard' or 'shit'. Lines such as 'She used to love me but now I am a crumb in the biscuit tin of life' can induce vomiting. 'She used to love me / My heart is the sound of oysters opening at low tide' can also be counted on to take the breath away.

Micturation syncope is a syndrome in which men who increase their intra-abdominal pressure at the moment of urination can impair their venous return, cardiac output and subsequently faint, however this cause will usually be obvious from the history and immediate setting. Individuals suffering in this manner can sometimes be confused with those who have drunk too much then pissed themselves before collapsing.

Despite a strong link between alcohol and poetry this scenario seems unlikely to be the case in your situation and so it only remains for me to write you the following prescription—four black wheels swallowed whole like pills; one siren, the blade of a sharp knife; three sheets, as crisp as biting apples, two flashing lights striking matches in the wind—and in this small ambulance send you, like flowers, straight to hospital.

JENNIFER COMPTON

The Threepenny Kowhai Stamp Brooch

If I get lost someone will pick me up and post me.
I am already licked and stamped on my green lapel.

The brooch from Te Papa will see me safely home.
It's 3^D—as in LSD—pounds, shillings and pence.

Let us go out and do the *passegiata* on the waterfront.
If and when I get lost, you can slide me into the red box.

Of course I will be posted back into the past—
back to when kowhai was pronounced kowhai.

MARY CRESSWELL

Golden Weather (Cook Strait)

Nana died on Boxing Day
we left Makara in kayaks

we paddled all night, we paddled away
Dad steered to the Southern Cross

we lashed the dog to a boogie board
and ate cold cheerios with tomato sauce

Porpoises played as we packed our sad
at dawn we skimmed the swells

the yellow Lab sank beneath the waves
Farewell, wept Mum, farewell.

At high noon Nana was bronzed
we swallowed grief and sausage rolls

Not before time we left for home
we turned our backs on the day

goodbye, we cried, you golden sun!
goodbye, goodbye, you yellow dog!

ALLEN CURNOW

When and Where

Where the big crowds come, the street,
the stadium, the park where the young
go crazy to the beat
and the heated bubble of the song,

thoughts running loose, I tell
myself, the years will have blipped past,
one by one the lot of us here present will
be gone into the dark. Someone's last

hour's always next, right here and now.
Deep under the bark of that great oak
my father's lifetime's told in rings, which grow
to outlive me too. Gently as I stroke

this child's head, I'm thinking, 'Goodbye!
It's all yours now, the season's crop—
your time to bud, and bloom, while my
late leaves wither and drop—'

And which day of which year
to come will turn out to have been
the anniversary, distant or near,
of my death? Good question. The scene,

will it be wartime, on a trip,
or at home or in some nearby
street, crashed coach or a ship-
wreck that I'm to die?

Cadavers couldn't care less where they rot,
yet the living tissue leans (as best it may)
toward the long-loved familiar spot
for its rest. Mine does, think of it that way.

Freshly dug. Young things, chase your ball.
Nature's not watching, only minding,
by its own light perpetual
beauty of its own fact or finding.

LYNN DAVIDSON

Before we all hung out in cafés

At primary school on the monkey bars
we'd hang, aching, from the middle rung

having riffed our way along the first six bars
then the wrench in the shoulders at the seventh.

Nowhere to go but the classroom or home
from the patch of rubbed out grass

where the rhythm failed us.

FIONA FARRELL

Our trip to Takaka

Well, we went to Takaka
for the weekend
and there was this spring.
Yes.
This spring.
And we could see under the
water with this mirror thing.
And there was this eel.
Yes.
This eel, swimming from right
to left like a reel of silk ribbon,
like a pennant waving.
You know: a pennant,
with teeth and an eye like a
silver stud among all this
pondweed. And there were
all these bubbles. Each one
was like a little world
rising in its sleek skin.
And then we went to see
the goldfields.
Yes.
Goldfields.
And there were these caves
in scrubland. They'd stripped
the hills till the ground ran red.
And we went into one of the
caves and there was this young
man sleeping on fern fronds,
meditating to make the world
well. He had his dog with him.
Yes.
His dog.

That's how we knew he was there.
The cave was deep, like an ear.
Or a belly button. It was deep and
damp, and we heard the dog bark
down in the dark and a young man
saying, 'Be quiet!'
The clay in the cave stuck
to our hands like dry blood.
We gave the young man a
bread roll.
Yes.
A bread roll.
With cheese and egg. And we
said, Well, good luck with the
meditating and everything.
He said, yeah, well, he was
going to give it his best shot.
And then we went home.
Yes.
Home.
The place where we live.

And I thought it seemed a little better.
Yes.
Just a little better.

After our trip to Takaka.

CLIFF FELL

Ophelia

For Guy Williams

1. *That moment*

There comes a moment
when you don't know where you end
and the creature in your arms begins.

The long rains.
Two years on from the accident
and the day after my sister left—
the day we knew we could be lovers no more
than sun and moon embrace the cradled earth.

I almost missed it in the market,
the monsoon slapping down,
but turned to see what I'd ignored:
wrapped in a faded, torn kikoy, a wriggle
and her hopeless eyes staring into me:

and all of Africa's anger and sex and wildness
were riding in there.

2. *The price*

And there she was—
a baboon,
I said—
and not one of the blue baboons
you find upcountry
but a golden baboon from the coast,
a six-week-old Monroe blonde
who was already in my arms,
her little hands fast around the buttons of my shirt.

Unotoka wapi?
(Where d'you get her?)
I asked the Giriama—
one of the untouchable bushmen
of the coast—
                              he'd shot her mother,
drugged her with arrows to feed alive
to his pet python

and I bought her there and then,
for a ten bob cheque
written in pencil
                              which bounced.

3. Her name

Why did I give her such a tragic name?
Perhaps it was the *Hamlet* I'd just done
but more to the point—at only fifteen
I guess I'd guessed what was to come;

and she as motherless as me
that when I stared into her eyes—
and it's this that I want to remember—
that look when you look into an animal

and see your own soul's country
deep in there, beyond the dark horizon.
And she brought me flowers, petals from the garden,
and her moon-coloured cries at night.

4. Food

Whatever I ate, she ate—and from my bowl:
stone-sized chunks of aloneness
and whatever else my father's allowance allowed.
Sometimes an arm of grass, poured on a silver plate
from which her shining black fingers deftly sorted

all the seeds, which she ate
like a queen, buzzing away to herself,
while I lay on the sofa
smoking.

5. *Tricks*

Tricks? Yes, she could do tricks:
she could outdrink anyone in the New Stanley,
pints of Elephant beer, though once
so drunk she jumped on Jack Block's head—
the owner deep in concentrated talk
trying to sell the place again.
Why him?
He banned us for ever then.

And her noise a wonder in my bed at night.

But it wasn't her tricks so much
as just her being there:
at the chai kiosks and foodcarts of River Rd.
we ate African for free
sikuma wiki, posho, mukate maiyai—
for the punters we brought in.

And once, her first time on heat,
I woke in the dark to find her
gently
            sweetly
wanking us off—
both of us together.

6. *Inner child*

Stare into her eyes—
the fires and shining greens, the night's bright gems.

Do we reflect each other? Yes, we reflect each other—
but I want to enter that look and live in there for ever
to know what the child inside her thinks of me
and this other country, this dream I've brought her to.

And we stared into each other's eyes—
        careless because we didn't care
        fearless because there was nothing to fear
        but the death we both inhabited

laughing as we waited for the final act—
        like I was her Player King
        and she my Player Queen.

7. *Abuse*

But it wasn't all roses.
Have you ever tried
to house-train a baboon?

Shit everywhere. In our bed
at night, in the kitchen:
the houseboy fled after two days.

The old soliloquies of abuse:
I cursed her, I wished her gone—
away into the prayers and habits of

white silence.
                        And was it physical abuse?

Yes, it was physical abuse:
I rubbed her face in it.
I beat her.
I locked her in the toilet

where Africa's tongue accused me,
screaming her wonderful noise.

8. *A story*

My little put-put, my 50cc Yamaha—
that's how she travelled, riding pillion,
clinging to my waist, slipped inside my shirt.

Langata Rd., 4 a.m.—army roadblock:
spikes and chains, and cavalettis on the road
like a riding school.

The soldiers relax around me, smiling:
Habari aku, bwana? Pleasantries of the black night—
no matter this mzungu on a bike.

Then, her tail twitches and stands up
on the seat behind me—like a rod: *Shaitani!*
Shaitani! Devil! and their guns all cocked at me.

'Hey, whoa . . .' holding to the softness in my voice.
'It's only my baboon'—and as always in Africa
the childlike roar of laughter at ourselves

and friends for life, for ever.

9. *What was to come*

The Ministry of Wildlife was on to me.
My friends were on to me. My sister
was on to me, and the houseboys.
Through it all, Ophelia muttered at nothing.
She picked the lice from my hair.
She brought me avocados from high up the tree—

their dark jade glowing in her shiny black palms,
in the creases of her fingers.

10. *For ever*

What is time to a baboon?

What did it mean to those eyes
that followed me from room to room,
or through the shantytowns
and Arab Quarter alleys
where children play soccer in the dust
and call for her, and follow her,
who followed me.

And even when she wasn't there,
when I locked her in the bathroom,
I could feel her gargoyle eyes on me,
the scrutiny that wildness grants—
to have this second sight with me.

But I don't know what time meant to her,
though if I had to guess
I'd say it meant simply this:
that we were there, together in that moment

and that the passing of each moment
was for ever, or is for ever
in the present simple tense to her.

11. *Husband*

I had to do something.
A 'husband' must be found for her.
A born-free solution. After all,
this was Adamson Land.

I took her to a farm in Macharkos—
Eden Hill. For three weeks I climbed
through trees with her,

teaching her to swing through them—
to teach her to survive.

And then I betrayed her twice on paper:
I divorced her with my signature.
I gave up such rights as I was said to have
and read again my traitor's name—
printed in carbon on a BOAC ticket,

bound for England.

12. Bees

Under the flyover, a council flat in Hammersmith,
where the letter came, falling like an autumn leaf,
wrapped in someone's white bandages.

It said that she'd been killed by bees,
stung to death,
trying to rob their honey.

I wept. I didn't want to believe.
I couldn't weep her out of me.
I wept her out of me.

13. Baboonery

Time knows many ways of passing.

A yew tree in the graveyard at Stoke Gabriel—
green smoke of its branches
hangs above the tombs.
Its roots are said to feed in every grave.

Carvings on the church door.
The gargoyle style
                    they call baboonery—

how is it I forget you,
Ophelia,
for all of thirty years?

I look up at the stone faces:
a worn-out Herne the Hunter,
the wild hunt searching for souls—

and hold you as I come into myself,
feeding on that moment

where I don't know where I end

and the baboon in my arms begins.

SIA FIGIEL

Songs of the fat brown woman
for sista grace (nichols) and the fat black woman

The fat brown woman move in the breeze
under the thatch of the small small fale
braiding sinnet
weaving stories
between the leaves of the pandanus

The fat brown woman sweat in the sun
lean on a coconut palm
swaying in the coconut sun
in colourful lavalava too small for her waist

The fat brown woman in the sea
is a sight to see
diving for blue fish red fish
an occasional eel
The fat brown woman walking home from the sea
is a sight to see

Around the fat brown woman there is
always a man or two
Big or small
Smiling smiling
At the way her hip sway
At the sound her thigh make
Around the fat brown woman there is
always a fly
or two
too

See the fat brown woman at a fa'alavelave
Directing the men the women
A fine mat here

A pig there
In her fat brown woman voice
in her fat brown woman style
gentle but firm
is the fat brown woman

When the fat brown woman hops on the bus the girls
and boys whisper
and men and women whisper
and children and cat whisper whisper
and pigs too sometimes
watch her sway
sway sway
and her arms moving like dat
and a shaking like dat
is her tummy too

they make room right behind the skinny
bus driver who gives her a big fat wink
the fat brown woman takes out a bright red
hanky wipes the sweat off her brow
pats her cheek
adjusts her dress/her bra/
her hip
chase away the flies
give the bus driver a mean look
Is going be a long way to market

So you can look all you want
And you can watch all you want
And you can stare all you want
But the fat brown woman will keep
swaying her hip
Keep swaying her hip
All the way to town

The fat brown woman watches miss universe on tee vee

What do you say is
going through the mind of the fat brown woman
watching miss universe the most beautiful woman in the
     world?
a aerobic instructa
wants to be a air hostess
a brain surgeon
perhaps
is her dream?
The fat brown woman add more coconut cream to the saka
and adjust her lavalava
call out to her big sista
e! we need to fix dat damn scale!

The fat brown woman's fat brown sista

Sits in the cool
of an air-conditioned room
directing an organisation
managing an institution
rewriting her constitution

Warning about the fat brown woman

The fat brown woman is quiet as you know
Doesn't say a word
An occasional laugh
She does not gossip
She does not lie
Will tell you straight away
Whether you sleeping with a fly
but piss the fat brown woman off and you see eyes
you never seen before
and a mouth you
never heard before
And if I was you I'd stay clear out of the way

Of the fat brown woman
When she's mad
When she's pissed
I'd stay clear out of the way
If I was you
I'd stay clear out of the way
Of whereva she going sit

A last note on the fat brown woman and shoes

No shoe fits the foot of the fat brown woman
No high heel
No low heel
No prince
No king
Can contain
Constrain
Confine the foot of the fat brown woman
Because the feet of the fat brown woman
Are grounded nicely to the bellies of
Her Mamas
The fat blue Pacific
The fat brown Earth
Thank you very much

JOAN FLEMING

Theory of light

Andy goes craving all over the beach
with her red grip and her red grapple.

A red apple after dark isn't red,
it's a black apple.

She says she'll black up if she doesn't have salt.
She finds a sea urchin full of holes.

What's a blue sea after dark?
Are these the spaces where breath goes?

I find a gorgeous gold-yellow branch,
a colour, a describable friend.

We carry our findings, our branches
and urchins, from end to end.

The blue and red and yellow everywhere
is our theory of colour, of light.

Young salt-footed fools, you know there are no ends,
only ends in sight.

RHIAN GALLAGHER

Burial

The shovels stood in a sticky underbelly of earth
as we stepped from the sidelines for him,
peeling our jackets, the boys loosening their ties.
Soon there was clay on our church-going gear
and his voice coming out of our childhood
coaching us to put our backs into it.
Flowers and fine words had never touched the man
like work, grunts behind a shovel's bite,
the clean sound of clods as we heaved them in. Digging,
we bowed in memory of his stooped solid shape.
The dark damp weight of earth,
a provision, a very last word.

JOHN GALLAS

the Mongolian Women's Orchestra

enter the Mongolian Women's Band
with
the years,

whose music, theirs and theirs, like language learned,
inevitable, red and super-sound,
outplays the days the days that made it mine

and beauty beauty adds to it—its stir,
its wink, its melt, and anything that shines—
this is The Horse that Overtook the Wind:

the little men that ride the plain
on hearts that will not race again
whose hoofbeats knock on heaven's door—
they will not come back anymore

the history of hope is short:
it has one chapter—Youth. I thought
that memories would make me wise
but nothing comes as no surprise

across the windy open spaces
briefly bright their shining faces
do with beauty then are gone—
the horses gallop on and on

and if I played my darndest, darndest card,
who have no beauty now, no more, what tricks
I take have not the hearts they had before.

The Horse that Overtook the Wind is done,
and beauty beauty raced it well—its stir,
its wink, its melt and anything that shines.

exit the Mongolian Women's Band
with
the years.

PAULA GREEN

Waitakere Rain

Ernest Hemingway found rain to be
made of knowledge, experience
wine oil salt vinegar quince
bed early mornings nights days the sea
men women dogs hill and rich valley
the appearance and disappearance of sense
or trains on curved and straight tracks, hence
love honour and dishonour, a scent of infinity.
In my city the rain you get
is made of massive kauri trees, the call of forest birds
howling dark oceans and mangroved creeks.
I taste constancy, memory and yet
there's the watery departure of words
from the thunder-black sand at Te Henga Beach.

BERNADETTE HALL

The History of Europe

It's heavy with lupin perfume, the rough
track. There's a shine on the claggy clay,
a double tyre track down the middle.

The pine forest looms like a collapsing
building. You half expect to see
two lost children, a slavering wolf,

an old woman gathering sticks in her apron.
Nothing moves. This is untrue.
Nothing appears to move but, in fact,

the purpley brown toadstools do
but imperceptibly, levering their little
round gun turrets up through the needles.

This is what happens.

Two men step out, silent in the silence,
one from each side of the dark that wells
in the dark of the pines. They stand

there braced like a locked gate.
Each one has a rifle across his chest
like a sash. It's the history of Europe.

Soon there will be dogs barking,
boots crashing through the matagouri.
Soon there will be shots and the rackety

clatter of a helicopter. Soon there will be
barked commands, bayonets and baying for blood,
someone in terror, trying to make a run for it.

DINAH HAWKEN

365 x 30

Lying on a bed with you
for at least
the ten thousandth time
I remember the dream
I had last night.

You and I and the young woman
you are going to marry
are in a shop
choosing a jacket for you
to wear at the wedding.
She chooses an absurd one
with taffeta panels on the front
and full gathered sleeves.
I see that your old one
the one you are wearing
is plain and smart. It suits you.

In the dream I do not speak
or act—I am there
as your friend, being reasonable
about the marriage—
but there is a distinct
holding in my shoulders
as if our days together
are taking a shape
that I am about to reach out
and raise
above all else

a double-handled jar
in which water turns to wine.

for Bill

SAM HUNT

Lines for a New Year

I like the branch
I find myself on

a view over the garden
all the way down to the beach

the family below me
gathered in the garden

debating where I've gone.
My father's got a theory.

I like the branch
I find myself on.

*

You know how it is

to give up the piss
a week to the

day before Christmas

you know how it is

to fall over sober
safe in some spot,

come to later
remembering the lot.

*

the rugby ball kicked
far as the far paddock

where an apple tree caught it.
Was agreed among folk

they'd never seen such a catch,
such a kick, such a match.

*

I gave it away lately
I had no choice,
no need pump the brakes—
they'd already seized.

I like your poison, lady,
I like it too much:
which is why I am
          where I am today
outside of thought, beyond your touch.

I said I'll be seeing you.
You knew what I meant,
at least you seemed to.
Was the message you got
the same one I sent?

*

It's a love song
between a mother and son.

The son plays the drums
and wrote the song.

On the recording
mother sings the song

like mothers do. And the
son plays the drums

like a good boy. It's a
love song.

*

A friend used to say
my dog and I
had the same way of walking,

especially walking away.
Which was
often the case.

These days there's
not much happening.
It's people walking toward me

asking, where's the dog,
the dog? And they're
right. Where is he?

*

You live in this world
you have no choice.
Silence would be fine.
But you give it voice—

you have to, you cannot
help yourself.
Your mother says you never knew
when enough was enough.

*

Dreamt I met Thomas Hardy
walking a local back road.
He was an old man
but coped okay with his cane.

He said he was looking for
a woman called Lizbie Brown.
I said I knew her name—
but only from his poem.

*

Sitting on a clifftop
was always a dream
that more or less came true.
Just the words dried up.

*

Friends disappear
off the face of the earth.
For what it's worth
I loved you.
But you can't hear.

*

Is said (what few
elders we have left)
anyone for whom birds sing
all night through to dawn

are themselves
close to eternal bird-song:
their time, among these branches,
that of the elders—not long.

*

If this were the view
I got all year through—
a branch of a tree at the window—

I would become that
branch of tree and with it
grow.

The nurses agree
I never complain
about the rain, or pain.

Easy, when you know
you're a tree
at the window.

*

When I poured her a cup of tea
and asked her, strong or weak?
she held out a dark wrist:
same colour as this.

*

I'm off to look at angels.
And toetoe if I see it.

The family move in close.
No way out but

close my eyes to see

if anything's left of the toetoe,
and the angels.

ANNA JACKSON

Spring

All day today the ice melted.
My name is Queen.
I haven't melted at all
though I am soft
and getting softer
until I will pardon you all.
I watch benignly as one by one
you slink off down diminishing avenues
to somewhere less central.
I pardon Jimmy who egged on Joe
who threw the snowball at Jean
and I pardon Jean for wiping off the snow
as if snow were something that should go.
Even the grass is pushing snow aside.
I can feel it rising up inside me, too.
I pardon it
and get on with my reign.

LYNN JENNER

Women's Business

When I had a son in his early teens
a Russian thought formed in my head
that if a war came I would cut off
the index finger of his right hand
so that he would be no use for fighting.
The part of me which visits
hospitals would do the cutting.
I wouldn't care if he hated me
for what I did.
I might even be pleased.
By this time I knew that he was nearly
a man, and that if I didn't cut his finger off
or shoot him in the foot, he would go.
Even if he was afraid.
Even if he thought it was pointless.
Now he is a man and I ask him
to carry my suitcase.

ANDREW JOHNSTON

The Sunflower
for Stuart Johnston, 1931–2004

One young bloom in a vase or jar, breath-
takingly yellow. And her
hands, in the morning light, the way
they arrange and rearrange. Death
brings lilies, but someone has sent a sunflower:
this is our penance, staring at the sun,
its blind eye, its ragged halo. The day,
in the end, took to its bed
before the day was over, taking thee
with it. Soon this flower, too, will be dead,
its summer of wondering done
about the sun, petal by petal: loved me;

didn't know how; did, unsayably so. It leaves me
as he left us, in the dark. From one breath
to the next, he'd deflect a question: in his the-
ology, *I, me, mine* were just not done.
Because he saw eye to eye with death
we can stare at the sunflower all day
but his heavenly father's garden was further
than we were prepared to go—its bed
of blood-red roses, its promises, its premises, the way
everything had been arranged; 'dead'
a manner of speaking, under the sun.
We counted ourselves lucky, hour by hour,

and by the minutes of the sunflower
(he doesn't, he does, he doesn't know me),
each in his or her own way worshipping the sun
and coming to other arrangements with death—
that it is the end, in the abstract. And then one day
someone calls, and you take a deep, deep breath.

Sister nor'wester, southerly brother—
into the mind of the man we guess our way,
blind and deaf, senseless, because he is dead.
From the end of the earth I will cry unto thee,
as daughters and sons have always done,
for words unsaid. The riverbed

was dry and I was thirsty. By your bed,
near the end, we could count our
blessings: each day,
for one thing, and though it was winter, the sun.
A sisterly sixth sense, when death
began to bloom, flew me
from the end of the earth. In a week you were dead
but we shadowed one another
through the brittle days before you went away.
You talked and talked, as you'd always done,
of all but you, till you were out of breath.
I would have liked to hear—despite your fear of the-

atre (so foolish was I, and ignorant, before thee)—
about your mother, for instance, who took to bed
when tempers rose; and how the sun
had burned a dead-
ly thirst into your father's breath;
but the hard facts I craved, my mother
knew, were the same stones, day
after day, that you buried in death-
ly silence, so that in this inscrutable way
you could build—for you, for her, for six including me—
a house, a plain, safe house, with a sunflower
in the garden. 'That which is done

is that which shall be done'
is all very well in the-
ory, but what if the sun
were black, and the book dead
wrong, and the interval under death

demanded a father
as unlike his father as day
and night? A breath
of wind reaches me
from the rose-bed;
in its vase or jar the sunflower
nods politely. Halfway

across the Channel, halfway
between waking and sleeping, my mind undone,
I had, as luck would have it, something of an inkling. The
    day
had been long; as I lay in the boat's narrow bed
a wave of black joy lifted me and left in me
knowledge so dark it shone. I held my breath.
Fear fell away, of death, and other
fears; the end, in the end, was the darkest jewel. I was dead
tired, and fatigue's mysterious flower
spoke perhaps in tongues. But that black sun
still shines—a talisman, obsidian, a bright antithe-
sis. Its darkness made light of death

at most, however, for me; the death
of someone else is something else. Your way
led over the border; I am a stranger with thee,
and a sojourner, but wherever I am, my place in the sun
you prepared. His earthly power
spent, your god, to us, is dead,
but it was your belief that gave us breath,
the life we take for granted every day.
What sense of your sense will I take with me?
How much of your world will we hand on?
Just before the end, on the wall beside your bed,
Peter pinned Leonardo's St. Anne. Her

smile, wry, reminds me of you, and her
hand-on-hip benevolence. Wherever death
leads, we can meet here. The power

of light in van Eyck and Vermeer. The breath
of Wallace Stevens, overhearing his way
to work. Every Henry James you read in bed,
destiny and destiny like night and day.
The valedictory music of 'The Dead'.
Thou hast set our iniquities before thee
but when all—or almost all—is said and done
sometimes it seemed you believed no less than me
that when we die we go into the sun.

There is nothing new under the sun
but much of it is mystery: this my mother knows. Her
psychological eye revised your the-
ological line. They'd converge, anyway,
at the library—your rain-cloud, your seed-bed.
You read and read and read. And saved your breath
not to write yourself, but to make each day
bloom and turn. The astonishing flower,
head full of edible seeds, bows down dead:
this is the credible sense of its death,
that here, where its turning is done
other journeys begin. It seems to me

you believed what you believed, but it strikes me,
too, that the seeds you sowed, in the mind's sun,
mattered most. (Sometimes they grew a bed
of nails: you were often 'sick to death'
of fads and feuds, the way
they shut out the sun.) Flower
of wonder, flower of might: if I see thee
on the other side, when I am dead,
I'll know there is an other
side. Till then, while we have breath,
our burgeoning work is not done:
what we have been given is a rich, difficult day

that could go on without us, nevertheless, all day,
whistling a cryptic tune. It comes to me

in the conservatory, where we catch a little sun:
I didn't know you well, and then you went away
but in the day of my trouble I will call upon thee
because you were a man to get things done.
In its vase or jar, the young sunflower
I imagine has served its purpose. Beneath its bed,
all along, the river was flowing—deep, where death
knows more than we. Sylvia dons her
gardening gloves to gather the dead
roses. Man cannot utter it, but under his breath:

'Remember me, my loves, when I am dead.'
Rest on memory's sea-bed: we will swim down to thee.
And in our own blue day, we will gaze at death
the way this one young bloom would gaze at the sun.
In the garden of the living, my mother stops for breath.
Thou thy worldly task hast done. And seeds rain from the
      sunflower.

ANNE KENNEDY

Die die, live live

1.

A puff of air
like a lover's
sweet speech
bubble, blue
as sky. A brown
horizon turning
fast into tomorrow
and tomorrow, etc.
Mud and leather
and a man
who runs like rubber
drawn from itself
over mud
born from
its muddy
mother field.
A kick-off
and the howl of
a moon's dog.
They kick
the tender thing and kick and kick the tender thing
and wail and sing.
Five-nil to them.
Fuck. And fuck
the conversion
too. More
points for them.
The ball sings.
The wind
sings a hymn
down the Saint

Patrick's Day
parade-length
of field
and the wind
blows the ball
where it shouldn't
go. You have to
hope these idiots
grasp softness
the idea of it
its air and
innocence.
Twelve-nil to
the other side.
Conversion? No.
A rose blooms.
The fullback
there he goes
into a scrum. He's
in the scrum
for his girlfriend
the girl he loves.
A torn ear a red rose the love-song of the fullback
a big man a
fucking giant
look at him
run. A lot of blood.
He runs for the
invisible woman.
He's a moving tree
a flowering
tree. The Aussie
should be sin-binned.
Oh. He is.
Penalty. Twelve-
three. Tenderness
and the terrible
wind-sound

necessary for
play. They kick the tender thing and kick and kick
the tender thing
and wail and sing.
A man jumps
to his feet
throwing the hand
of his girl into
the sky. He flails
and beseeches.
Go go go go go!
It's her envoi.
A guttural
call Moss has
never heard before
coming from
here and here
a beating on
the edge of seagull
i.e. clarinet.
There's a rolling
maul, players
scragging faces
with sprigs. The referee
runs and blood
runs like tears.
Penalty. Twelve-six.
Go man boot
the groaning
air cradle it
as your child.
Don't fucking
drop it idiot.
A moan goes up.
It rests in
the bodied
stadium staying
there, living on

among the people
as damage.
They kick the tender thing and kick and kick the tender
    thing
and wail and sing.
Rain starts. Good
for the home team
(used to it).
The visitors gnash
their teeth. Mud
sprays men
into fossils
memento mori.
They're covered
in the game
head to foot.
Outrageous penalty
fifteen-six. Fuck.
A scrum in mud
and more rain.
The field is
ankle-glass
sometimes shattered as a dance once seen moved in water
a splish and trail
like scarves.
Half time
(FW).

2.

The land shaved
of trees made
useful by
its nakedness
and water. Men
stand as if cattle
mirrored at
a trough. A whistle

like a cast
in a roving
eye roving
over the field.
The men swarm
towards the ball
flicking earth
and sky.
The Centre's
butchering
down the field
as a lion hunts
prey in the late
afternoon.
As a boy he
loved animals.
Off-side. Fuck.
Blood and
sweat and blood
and the crack
of bones. They kick the tender thing and kick and kick
the tender thing
and wail and sing
and wail and sing.
A man is carried
off by St John's
Ambulance. Ah well
Fifteen-eleven
but missed the
conversion the
egg. Another
kick-off and
before long
a line-out whatever
that is. A player
hurling himself
into infinity
running and falling

and not caring
his body everything
and nothing
hovering
on the brink of
his death, death
of a small
nation. He is
a carcass
or palace. He's carried off by St John's Ambulance.
But there's a penalty.
Fifteen-fourteen.
They kick
the tender thing
and kick and kick
the tender thing
and wail and sing.
Howl and a face
coated in the season
and the game
is a season
imperative
compulsory
gone again and
a girl who walks into a woman. And rain drums the length
of rain
drumming.
It's late
and the sun dips
below the cap
of cloud touching
the heads of
the crowd limning
a moment blue.
They kick
the tender thing
and kick and kick
the tender thing

and wail and sing.
On the field
blood squelches
underfoot.
Twenty-fourteen.
Paul weeps
on her shoulder.
They've lost.
If they'd won
there'd be
just the same
weeping like a
well a stream
or cataract. She holds his bones under her hands
his back
where wings
might once
have been.
A good man
full of tenderness
giant i.e. a lot of
tenderness.
The small mercy
of no conversion.
A minute to go.
A man runs
down the field
like a doctor
in a field hospital.
A try to us!
Forty seconds
to go. The
half-back
lines up the
wet egg
of the universe
and after some
deliberation kicks

the tender thing.
And wails.
And sings.
Converted.
The sun sinks
The whistle blows.
They won!
(i.e. We won
apparently)
Paul and his mates
leap to their feet.
Hell we won.
They leap one
by one. Fintan
leaps to his feet.
Look even
Forest is leaping
to his feet. Moss
carried away with
the win and
Paul weeping
and giants leaping
and without thinking
she stands.
She looks down
at the long body
her old favourite.
And glances up
at the great giant
there beside her
a head taller
(no matter, he will
soon go away now
the game is over
and there is just
Finnegans Wake
to read or whatever
tall tale it was).

Light from
the tall lamp casts the giant shadow of the girl over Paul.
He is bathed
in a quick new
coolness, as
dusk falls suddenly
in the Tropics
and feels it
and stares up
at the girl and
backs and backs
(the love song
of the full-back).

MICHELE LEGGOTT

nice feijoas

sometimes you meet the title
walking home and the first lines
present themselves at the corner
as you turn and the low slant of the sun
means they haven't turned off
daylight saving this year though
the computers switched yesterday
and we fell back not even noticing
the difference   dark mornings
for long evenings   a good trade
but the sign at the neighbour's gate
goes out on tree time and that's
the tuning to set feet walking
over the easily deceived surface
of the waking mind   gold coins
for bags of fruit by the blackboard
under the jacaranda   the clock
at the gate the clock on the screen
and somewhere between them
whatever it is to be done as the day
shakes a leg and the heart puts up

its fun   *September's Baccalaureate*
a perfect mirror from somewhere else
crickets crows and retrospects   that view
we swim towards in the flat blue water
full of mangrove seeds and the bities
that get between lycra and skin
when the sea is warm and the moon
flies up each night towards Easter

they thought the dog might not
pull through a night to forget
I carried her in my arms when she
could not walk and someone
on the other side of the park
gave us a ride to the clinic   a drip
and many gold coins later
she is ok and the cnidaria stings
have worked their poison out
of our unlovely hides   everyone
sleeps better and is looking forward
to hot cross buns   the togs drip dry
washed out with soap to eliminate
the locomotion of jellyfish
and the poet philosophers turn back
to their elegant connection
of continents and light

GRAHAM LINDSAY

big bed

Close the little papa's eyes,
close'm eyes, close'm eyes.

Sleepy baby with the goldfish lips,
deep dark lashes, angel-pink cheeks,

ears like truffles, or hatchcovers
for underground shelters.

Darling baby with the snotty snout,
swept-back 'in flight' hair,

the tightly closed lashes
of a president embalmed

in a coffin of dreams, under the eye
of the gaudy activity bear,

Ellis's *Arepa Omeka*—
a tattooed, rope-wristed

hand and a fish—
the poster of Barney and friends.

The curtains shuffle in an easterly.
Tamarisk feathers fade yellow, fade green

in a sea of moist air and chimney pots.
Not a palace, but cheerful,

this little house and warm.
We have an angel in the bed with us:

chafed fluey nostrils and wide
globed brow, his right arm flung

between her face and mine,
the left left out on the covers.

Spider-red capillaries on shut lids,
Chanel lips succulent as anemones,

nipple-blistered still at twenty months.
Her ring-finger hand covers one breast.

He sucks the other and fiddles
with my penis with his foot.

ANNA LIVESEY

Shoeman in Love

I fell in love
through a pair of beaded slippers.

She brought them to me
to have the heels repaired.

They were black satin,
the toes hung with jet beads

and lined with pig-skin,
a leather that absorbs sweat.

Her voice was like pig-skin,
fine and strong enough

to absorb me,
but it wasn't that—

it was the taste
of the imprint of her heel

when I licked it,
holding her slipper

in front of my face
like a cup.

CILLA MCQUEEN

Ripples

The computer is dead; long live the computer.
In the meantime I write by hand.

Across the road has appeared a For Sale sign
in long grass beside the toetoe in the empty section.
In the middle distance, wind-burned iron roofs chafed by
    macrocarpa,
wooden power poles, manuka, the Challenge garage,
cars on the bridge
to the island harbour, containers, cranes, warehouses,
fishing boats, ships.

Stockpiled woodchips, tawny forests piled like salt.
Moon-grey sheep-fold in a stony pasture.
The far shore underlines blue mountains.
Across the harbour against the sinuous ranges
stands a white and grey Lego block,
the new milk powder plant, fifteen minutes on the arc by
    road
from here to there. When my eyes sweep the horizon
they come across a Lego block where there was none.

In the slow ground boulders grow.
Silvered timbers fold the sheep.
Cloud cliffs over Konini, five miles high from west to east.
Agate pebble in my palm
feels like rhyme to my warm skin.
Five dimensions coiled inside, colour deepened by my
    tongue.

I see Hone with clarity.
The bronze sheen of his skin,
tapering fingers, hand on my arm.

He might be just up the road at Kaka Point.
Alone within alone.
Petrified whalebone.

Tui twangs, triggers ripples.
Under the wilding branches magnified sepia leaf-shadows
play on viridian mosses, rusty iron, ferns, rotten logs.
Pile dead branches and jump on them.
In shade and shattered light dull logs crack, twigs snap.
Floored with leaf-mould, fern, deep loam, this is the hut.

In koromiko shade an iridescent diagram,
fine landing strip, concentric trap,
text between twigs, arachnid syntax,
parlour game in a gossamer field
of forty radii, seven anchors, three strong horizontals.
Along these lines slide spectral parallactic gleams.

I fell in the window. He was asleep in front of the potbelly.
Deaf smile, shining-eyed surprise—
I was afraid you might have burned your legs.
After the funeral service you leaned down towards me out
    of a cloud;
'Kia mau!' you shouted into my mind.

You might be talking with Joanna.
There she is in a red coat arriving on the ferry.
I watch her painting watercolours. Colours bless the paper.
'A shape to part the space,' she smiles, 'Morandi.'
Quietly, she is gone.

Dawn or dusk? I can't quite hear what they are saying,
I can't get a handle on them, they pull away like water.
Swirling kelp wind, cabbage trees green-faced wildcats.
The house bangs like a cardboard box.
It's calm in here.
Some shells empty, some shells full.
My friends talking quietly, just out of ear-shot.

Mist fills the harbour.
Only the tip of the smelter chimney is showing,
a black accidental on white. The long wharf juts hatched
    across nothing.
Straight lines and clustered blocks, taupe, beige, aluminium,
blend with the sand, sea, isabelline sky.

I was astral travelling.
Set in the middle knuckle of his hand
a round World, deep blue and green, a jewel,
a navigation device.
He stretched his arm and we flew beyond the Last
    Scattering,
beyond the primal molecules
where Nothing warps at the approach of light.

Soul wrapped in a mystery.

Don't worry, when the planet is completely wrecked

the seas will deepen for a time until they disappear in mist
and we are left like Mars.
The last of us might carve some mighty lines in Earth
like Nascar lines—or Boreray—scrape off the turf
to leave a message on the hill, visible from Hirta—
great navigation lines that point through space
to join with other lines,
our landing strips on some green other world.

There is no malice in the computer,
nor inclination towards good.
In language ether particles form;
word behaviours give thought tongue
in codes and keys—

Then there is an earthquake.
The kitchen cupboards judder as if a tractor drove across
    the roof

windows struggling panes/ what if/ disrupted/ the
    cupboards
tumbled/ the piles
collapsed/ the tidal wave impending/ giant broccoli/ without
    malice/ keys and codes in tongue
Certainly uncaring. I need Bell tea, for Earl Grey is insipid.
In the kitchen hot teabag juice through fingers,
dropped in the sink a dry bud.

Cosmic code winks on power lines after the billions of rain.
Legs piston past on the white Staffy, Oscar.

Bidibids, snags, pulled threads,
flaws in the weave, points de repère.
Can't be sure of molecules making us up momently
whose memory expands with time
and over time the mind
caught on a detail, thorn, spark, madeleine, opening
a bubble
torus
wormhole;
via chance harmonics,
pools of connection, shocks and ripples,
traversing dimensions.

A shape to part the space—

The edges are shy and to be approached with caution
lest they lose their inner concentration, become self-
    conscious
in the Adam-and-Eve effect
slip through a gap, perhaps,
change phase—subject to object,
innocence to experience, perhaps.

So   turn stone
    over
                on the tongue.

SELINA TUSITALA MARSH

Not Another Nafanua Poem

Not another nafanua poem she can hear them say as she
attempts to ride the current of her culture in the new
millennium with her electric waka I'm afraid so her shadow
answers back in black but this ride's for nua's sister the one
who stayed home and fed her father koko alaisa wiping
his chin and fetching the key for the cupboard holding the
toilet pepa for the faleuila outside while her famous warrior
sister slay the stereotypes on an oceanic scale I'm afraid
so because this is the story of how her sister had to replace
the stolen coconuts meant for that evening's saka that the
warrior took without asking to cover her womanhood I'm
afraid so because someone had to feed the aiga harvest the
kalo the bananas the pawpaw bagging them and dragging
them to makeke fou to sell for kupe to pay the government
school for the kids to get a scholarship up and out of here
so they can come back and open a restaurant in apia and
finally begin to tap into those rivulets of capitalism spilling
over and into the sewers and into the streets and into the
back roads of the kua back villages except for nafanua's
village someone has to tell said the shadow.

KARLO MILA

Sacred Pulu

let me rip off
your images
and write about the bleeding beetroot pink purity
of Cook Islands potato salad
melting into subtropical mango horizons,
let me crap on poetically papaya
inhaling the bottle blonde fragrance of gardenia
let me pop some pods of vanilla
and talk dried banana bullshit

let me write about
the mountains of Manu'a
from the flats of Mangere town centre
let me shower you
with falling frangipani fakeness
$2 a lei from a Chinese shop in Otahu
let me keep it real
with the bitterness of lime from Foodtown $15.99 a kg
for raw fish ota ika perfection

let me bowl you a type of stereo
that sings lotto-ad-styles
hula hip hop
wop de fob
fresh fresh fresh
out of the deep freeze

let me scream a Niuean chant
like Xena
and slap my chest ma'ulu'ulu style
till my Wonderbra sings like a coconut
let me siva you away like Sosefina
last song, feeling up the dancefloor

let me romanticise us
away from
the grubby white sneaker existence
stuck to chewing gum of Otara markets
carried into the CBD of Saturday night
the fruit is so bright
we need shades
Gucci
electric windowed over blood burst eyes
still leaking with the ecstasy of last night

let me write about
doing the do
that hasn' t been done
to death
quite yet
with a little help from high street friends
black grace on white powder
so nesian mystical

yes, look up from your pokey poverty
and get angry about this poem
you're always a gold coin koha
away from winning lotto
one lotu away
from the salvation day
and yes
we're halfway between
buttnaked and never-never land
Hawaiki
it's a trip
I've never been able to save for
I tell you
stuck in rainy days all the time
Hawaiki
so far a lave lave away
from us all

STEPHANIE DE MONTALK

Hawkeye V4

She leaves her shoes at the door

*

dresses in blue

*

and bares her vein
for the radioactive tracer
which, inherently unstable,
will almost certainly
collapse in on itself
and begin to break down.

*

Above, the unforgettable name
of the machine.

To her left, a panel
of cobalt, crimson and gold:
a sideshow should
the power supply fail.

To her right, coded instructions
should the computer
and irresistible chemistry
develop a stammer
or taste for adventure.

*

Feet first, she slides
into the revolving hum
of the camera—

sun one minute,
stars the next—

and, courtesy of the control room,
National Radio with
the trial testing of toxic gases,

fewer groceries
in the family basket

and the News Headlines at Twelve
counting down
to Microsoft's warning
of a critical flaw
in its software.

EMMA NEALE

Brooch

Once I discover my father has given
a favourite eighteen-year-old medical student
a silver pin
crafted like an aeroplane
and a cheque for two nights' accommodation
in Las Vegas
with a handwritten card that says
'I wish you well in your public life,
wish to support you in your first flight from home,
I feel this cheque is generous,'
and I watch his hand, surprisingly slender,
the gentle hunch of his shoulders,
his quiet self-smile,

I wonder why I've never met this girl
who I learn has hair the colour of cigarillo papers,
voice soft as moccasins,
skin the colour of late magnolia,
her clothes the blue that winter shadows dye the ground

and why now I wake myself from this dream
with the belief that the sound of weeping
must come from the empty bedroom
down the hall.

JAMES NORCLIFFE

yet another poem about a giraffe

pity the poor giraffe
lost on the frozen steppe

his wishbone legs
make pipe-holes in the snow

the stunted furze
laughs at his reaching neck

for Africa is
sixty degrees below

the hoarfrost catches
in his soulful lashes

his brown eyes lost
beneath the arctic moon

his blotched hide a map
of hopeless wishes

the swishing tail
a pendulum of doom

so he stands withstands
the bitter polar blast

that rips the fluttering
pages of his dreams

the flickering pixels
of a brilliant past

when the world was warm
and still and green

GREGORY O'BRIEN

Where I Went

I auditioned for the part. And this way
I came to dance
to a confusion of heartbeat monitors and

portable radios. And so it fell upon me
to be the singing one
in a room given too much to silence.

In the intermittent light I was
speckled and
free. At the far end of each jaded afternoon

I was a six-foot dispenser of
effervescent drinks.
The ward was in need of a popular song

and I was it—a sponge to remove
unnecessary detail
from the ceiling so no one

was reminded of a world before
this one. I was
the overflowing one in the parched room.

And beside the far bed I was a student
of an Austrian architect
a pair of sunglasses grazing the night sky.

For him I wrote 'Vienna' across Evans Bay.
But in the morning
he told me, it was the designs of Maori buildings

I wore upon my chin. I was light-footed
in the crippled room
where the floor stared up at me

an ensemble of coloured things, my words
a cloth to soak them up
or remove them. Later I emptied

all the instruments of their music
like fruit, then I emptied
any other thing that might contain

music. I stayed all night in the day room
and the night stayed
with me. I was its furniture, its sweeping broom,

ninety per cent song and ten per cent flesh
of its body. I was paid
to weep in the laughing room and laugh

in the room of diminished hope. I was
the ripe one
in the spoiled room, where it fell upon me to dispense

glasses of water and ceilinged sky to the
recently awakened
and to those who awaken each day

with a fresh skyscape sewn across the surface
of their heads. These men
and women who could see through me.

I brought them the brightest drinks, the most
iridescent straws
and the coloured shadows that fell upon

their throats as they drank were both the last
shadows of a fiery world
gone out and a reflection of

the next to come. When I left the dying room
I was the shape of everything
into which I had been poured.

And the room behind me was empty
and I was filled
to overflowing with it, where I went.

PETER OLDS

Disjointed on Wellington Railway Station

Where the night ends & the pallid day begins
several dirty old groaners lie & stand around
the railway station. One sleeps, a boot under
his head, a plastic shoulder bag clutched to his
belly, his pants half down exposing a white bum . . .

I sit on a kauri bench & light up a Capstan,
place a boot on my rolled-up sleeping bag
& a free hand on top of my canvas pack.
A skinny man with a battered nose drops down
beside me, requests a smoke—his red eyes
unpicking my duffle coat, travelling over my
tennis shoes to the tailor-made cigarette in my hand.
'Non-filter,' I say—
'Better than nothin' his reply.

I light him up & give him half of what's left of
the pack (about five) which he tucks away on the
inside of his overcoat, then runs a hand over
his smooth grey hair—the only tidy part of him.
Two mates stand off talking with another guy:
secret laughs, hands in pockets, knowing nods.
An air of deliberate disjointedness. Last night's
close shave. An agreement to rendezvous
at an early opener later. Nervous like stage-fright
children ill at ease in a moneyed world . . .
They produce a bottle of sherry, which gets my mate
off the seat like a shot—but they don't want
to give him a drink.

Seems he played up last night, allowed himself
to get done over by the boys—took a lot of shit
on himself. The sight of him turns the others away—

seeing themselves in his snot-smashed face, blubbery
lips & puffy eyes.
They drink the sherry, smiling, rolling back on flat
heels like heroes having come through a horrific
night unscathed.

Another man in cowboy hat joins them, all belly
& beard, carrying a guitar. Wears moccasins—long
grey frizzy hair poking out from under the hat's
brim, an intelligent twinkle in the eye.
But when he opens his mouth & speaks his previous
demeanour changes from something strong & sure
to something weak & gone. His speech practically
unintelligible.
One asks the cowboy where he slept last night & he
somehow conveys 'Here' (at the station). He gets
the poor bastard look . . .

Suddenly, they take off on separate paths (in case
they're followed) toward the city centre, to meet up
later for tea at an all-night shelter.
My mate with the cigarettes tucked into his chest
waves a gloved hand (but not too revealingly) &
disappears in a swirl of railway grit . . .
The next time I see him (on Courtenay Place) he's
battered more than ever, looking like he's been
rolled. Clothes ripped, hair dishevelled, wild pale
eyes, paranoid pallor—charging apologetically
through the clean crowds heading God knows where
from God knows what.

BOB ORR

Eternity

Eternity is the traffic lights at Huntly—
before they change from red to green
I am lost in the enchantment of an ancient entertainment.
A wraith-like old wooden two-storey hotel
a war memorial hall with a padlocked front door
the sour taste on my tongue of a dust and diesel railway
    station
miners' cottages pale as mushrooms in the mist
a seesaw in the playground of a primary school
like scales that tilt toward injustice—
all become fantastical and floating
like some surreal craft now cut adrift by phantom boatmen.
Tilted on the river's broad traverse
the topsy-turvy of its history
down a surface cross threaded and riddled with mysteries
wide from its flashing underbelly
its streetlights like a gorse bloom's yellow carnival
through coal black waters voyaging this corridor of stars.
Do I merely chance to catch a glimpse of Mum and Dad
after a day out at the races
waltzing on the balcony of the Waipa Hotel—
Dad with his pockets full of fancy
the town's wake of champagne corks and ribbons
Mum laughing as he murmurs something?
All these years later in a midsummer night's dream
as I'm saying hullo and saying goodbye to them
waiting at the traffic lights as Huntly floats downstream.

CHRIS ORSMAN

Making Waves
for Maurice Wilkins

Light diffracted on a bedroom wall
at 30 Kelburn Parade, making waves
through a cloth blind, circa 1920;
outside, pongas and cabbage trees
lie just within memory's range,
a pattern and a shadow.
The silence here is qualified
but it draws you out, four years old,
or five. The world's a single room
where fronds and wind tap a code
against the window pane.

Next up you're wild, sprinting down
a helix of concrete steps
from the hills to the harbour.
Or you're leaning into a gale
commensurate to your incline
and weight; the elements support you,
and the blustery horizon
is fresh with new information.

*

And now the landscape changes
from island to continent to island again,
and there's a sea-change as we fire off
certain rays to form a transverse
across your history.
                    Acclimatised,
you wintered over in laboratories
and made a virtue of basements
and arcane knowledge; you found

a scientific silence or a calm
in which things are worked out
at a snail's pace, a slime
stretched and scrutinized between
forefinger and thumb to yield
a feast of the truth, or a field
ploughed with frustration, if that
is where our guesses land us.
For Science is a railway carriage
rocking with big ideas, sometimes
stalled on the sidings or slowed
on branch lines near rural stations.
And still the whole is too huge for us
to comprehend, one metre long,
wrapped around each cell,
unread until it's unwound,
the scarf and valence of our complexity,
from which we derive our unique timbre
to say: *Well done! Well done!*

*

To an amateur an x-ray plate
looks like an old fashioned
gramophone disk: yet it plays
scratchy music of the spheres,
jazz of an original order.
Or perhaps it's the ground-section
of a Byzantine cathedral, or a basilica
of double colonnades and semi-circular apse
—and who builds upwards from that
to discover the grand design? Who
constructs with only a floor plan
to find the elevations?
                              Those
who are neither architects nor masons
but quiet archaeologists of the unseen
hand and mind of God, digging upwards

to the exquisite airy construction
of the double helix. Gifted clumsiness?
Genius? You are there at the start of it,
a chiropractor of the biophysical,
clicking the backbone of DNA into place.

VINCENT O'SULLIVAN

The Child in the Gardens: Winter

How sudden, this entering the fallen
gardens for the first time, to feel the blisters
of the world's father, as his own hand
does. It is everything dying at once,
the slimed pond and the riffling of leaves,
shoes drenched across sapless stalks.
It is what you will read a thousand times.
You will come to think, who has not stood
there, holding that large hand, not said
Can't we go back—I don't like this place.
Your voice sounds like someone else's. You
rub a sleeve against your cheek, you want
him to laugh, to say, 'The early stars can't hurt
us, they are further than trains we hear
on the clearest of nights.' We are in a story
called Father, We Must Get Out.
Leaves scritch at the red walls,
a stone lady lies near the pond, eating
dirty grass. It is too sudden, this
walking into time for its first lesson,
its brown wind, its scummed nasty
paths. You know how lovely yellow
is your favourite colour, the kitchen at home.
You touch the big gates as you leave,
the trees stand on their bones, the shoulders
on the vandaled statue are huge cold
eggs. Nothing there wants to move.
You touch the gates and tell them, We
are not coming back to this place. Are we, Dad?

VIVIENNE PLUMB

Goldfish

My son doesn't go to school
any more he goes somewhere
else. He goes out walking alone
with his hat on his head,
lies on a bed, where they slip
a drip to the vein and
he has his body pumped full.
Funny how they grow up
says the woman who is the chemist,
Is it your only one?
It's harder then because you've spoilt them
here's your prescription, forty nine dollars.
I try to pretend
she doesn't know a thing, a thing that she's saying.
Here's a red light outside
and I have to stop, and everywhere there's children
a reminder of the way we come
into the world, birth, growth,
and end up fat or thin.
He, my own, was thin before
the drugs set in and made him fat,
now he looks like a frog.
There's a dog on the way home
so I pat it, sign of the hope
I have for the future.
When I get in he's on the bed
I can tell he feels bad, *don't*
he says. He often says that.
Or *come here* and he holds my
hand and there we are, two
tiny pebbles perched on the edge,
with the silvery sand far below us.
We don't like to use the C-word

says one white coat.
They prefer the ambiguous
nodes to *tumours*, or even
bumps and lumps, if you were dumb
you might think you had mumps.
In ward one he starts to tell me
his dream: we are chased
by a giant goldfish, we reach
a cellar, we are trapped
by the goggle-eyed fish in a dead
sea end, and then suddenly
he is all alone with an enormous
tome on his lap, the words *medical
dictionary* are embossed on its cover,
and he opens it, and he begins to read.

CHRIS PRICE

Rose and fell

Moist geometry unfurls.
      Dawn flushes the birds
from their silence

—hectic petticoats trimmed
      with disappearing mist—
and there, under a shaggy hem

      of pines, the monster Grendel
stealing home, mouth full
      of pinking shears.

His rough palm grips the bruised
      root of a plant torn
from a mountainside

      releasing scent of a more
legendary bloom.
               His pelt

glistens, the girl's words
      trapped moths
in his uncomprehending ears.

Wings of flowers
       fall and star
the path behind him

      as he travels
swiftly over the ground
      breathing   breathing.

KERRIN P. SHARPE

like rain the thunder

inside the tall gothic church
a man kisses the pieta

max is at the organ
composing a creation hymn

called apple and snow
all night the wind

wraps itself around the city
like a bell that does

not ring in danger but prayer
and genya's voice

falls from a clock
as she calls her children

kazia, stefan, hendrich, janek
her hand closes around

a winter apple
and somebody probably kazia

puts the kettle on
then all four children

gather their shadows
and become birds

MARTY SMITH

Hat

Dad wouldn't be seen dead
without a hat.
Farm hat, summer hat, town hat
even when he had hair.

Hat on an angle, hat on horse,
hat in the truck with dogs.

We fished by stealth
stalked trout
with a spear and a light.
He wore his hat in the dark.

A mile apart by metal road
my grandmother lived
on her half of the farm.
No chance meetings, not even
a skyline sighting.

She lay in wait in town
watched
from the haberdashery
as he walked up the street.
She came out as if by accident.
Hand frail, and clasping
the front of her coat,
she gave a coy look
from the bags of her bloodhound eyes—
the whole air stopped

he raised his hat, went past.

ELIZABETH SMITHER

Two security guards talking about Jupiter

Four little canvas bags of takings, one float, one
cash box and two guards to open the security room
where the squat safe is waiting. End of day ritual

but tonight they are talking of Jupiter
in male fashion. Did you see that
TV programme? About what the Earth

will be like when it dries out? A prune
sinking in on itself, a dust bowl falling
inwards like the orchestrated blowing up

of a building that comes down on the
spot ordained. Jupiter, on the contrary,
is a crystal planet. How strange, fitting

the cash bags in, pushing the cash box back
turning the handle so the teeth of the door mesh
and the maker's gold seal glows in the light

then finally the long thin key that someone
locked in the room might turn to open
to take out the bags and play with the money

but be unable to escape because the door
is deadbolted. Walking away, thinking
how like a little safe this planet is

locked tight, we trust, for the night
its systems meshed. Earth preserved in its
abundant waters, Jupiter in its dark moonlets.

C.K. STEAD

Without

Crossing Cook Strait
going home to be
ordained in the

parish of his
father, while seas wished
by and the wind

had its say in the
wires, it came to
him there was no

God. Not that
God was sulking or had
turned His back—that

had happened
often. It was that God
wasn't there, was

nowhere, a Word
without reference or
object. Who was

God? He was the
Lord. What Lord was
that? The Lord God. Back

and forth it went while
stern lifted, screw
shuddered, stars glowed

and faded. The
universe was losing
weight. It was

then he threw his
Bible into the
sea. He was a

poet and would
write his own. Happiness
was nothing

but not being
sad. It was your
self in this one and

only moment
without grief or
remorse, without God

or a future—sea,
sky, the decks
rolling underfoot.

RICHARD VON STURMER

After Arp

Mushrooms

The flat, black mushrooms
grow luxurious green hair.
Green hair edged
with a band of white.
Green hair as luminous
as underwater plants.
Green hair that can be fashioned
into horsehair whisks.

The flat, black mushrooms
exhale clusters of stars.
They live in a section of the forest
where no flies can settle.

*

The Great Slug

The great slug rides his bicycle.
His baggy pants can barely contain
his baggy pants.
He leaves behind
a trail of gray foam.

The great slug is a connoisseur
of sofas and lazy boy recliners.
He merely rides his bicycle
to rid himself
of certain metallic parasites
which inhabit the deeper recesses
of his sagging flesh.

If only the great slug
were a hermaphrodite.
But his penis
remains firmly fixed
in the centre of his forehead.

The slug and I have a long history
of altercations.
He's nothing but an impostor,
a provocateur,
a guzzler of kerosene.
Someday we'll settle old scores.
Someday we'll slug it out.

*

The Lozenge Box

fire of flamingos
smoke of bats
ash of ants

On one bleak
mid-winter's day
you offered me
the key to the lozenge box
and ever since then
multicoloured pastilles
continue to tumble out.

a flywheel
a watering can
Fidel Castro's
fountain pen

Multicoloured pastilles
continue to tumble out.

*

The Empress of Emptiness

What a belle,
what an absolute
fashion plate.

The Empress of Emptiness
puts on her tinsel crown
while the black bluejays
attack her battlements
with toothpicks
and tape recorders.

Serious tinnitus is sweeping through
Tintagel Castle
and Titus has gone to ground.

The Empress of Emptiness
gathers together her long dress
and disappears
down the elastic corridor.

*

My Uncle

My uncle
the acquirer of spoons
blind as a bat
skimming over the Astroturf.

Old polaroids
lie scattered like tiles
in his abandoned garden.

For a joke he once placed
a small, cloth sailor
inside a condom.

My uncle
who would break into a sweat
at the sight of a dead matchstick.

He loved the air
the letter H
the sound of castanets.

My uncle
who hypnotized
the King of Thailand

When I open the door
to his garden shed
sparrows fly out
from the rusted hinges.

*

Elephants

Elephants are never
irrelevant.
They use adjectives
to extract
honey from honeycombs.

*

Dinosaurs

It's wrong to compare ourselves with dinosaurs.
Dinosaurs didn't use power tools.
Dinosaurs didn't do jigsaw puzzles.

Dinosaurs never put a man on the moon.
They tore each other to pieces
and fell into tar pits.
It's wrong to compare ourselves with dinosaurs.

*

André Breton's Inflatable Octopus

André Breton's inflatable Octopus
occupies a portion of Belgium.
On Google Earth you can see the way
it sprawls across Brussels
with one tentacle reaching Antwerp
and another touching Ghent.

André Breton had a penchant
for anal eroticism.
On the other hand
his inflatable octopus
is not only immaculate
but ready, willing and able
to release a magnificent cloud
of perfumed ink.

*

Circadian Rhythms

Tapping on a toadstool
the sun comes up.

The crickets chirp
as they go to work
their little briefcases
filled with sesame seeds.

Tapping on a capped tooth
the moon goes down.

Slipped into a black folder
then filed away
deep in the archives
with all the other moons.

*

Our Ancestors

They found a billiard table
embedded
at the centre of an iceberg,
proof that our Neolithic ancestors
engaged in recreational activities.

The skeletons of hairy mammoths
still bear the scars
of their billiard cues.

And look—
over the horizon
kicking up the tundra
a great, enraged herd
of magnetic wildebeest!

*

Captain Cook's Hat

There's a tree growing
on Captain Cook's hat
two trees in fact,
one on the top
and one on the side.

The erratic navigator
likes to swim
with his dorsal-finned compass

and the blue almond sky

and the blue almond sky.

ROBERT SULLIVAN

After the UN Rapporteur Supported Maori Customary Rights

If it was tattooed in Maori there'd be an indigenous
Universe in this curvy groove—but it's a problem
of bleeding translation, to spit the worldview
from a disembodied tongue, no shy body, no sway—
a paintbrush tongue over eyes, face, hupe-nose
and wide toes, broad brow (that me you're picturing,
eh?), but Maori prose—that first named the land—
is wahangu, muted. The verbs, nouns, adjectives,
tenses, all the key teeth thrown on the table
are English played with by ancestors of Westminster

& Trickster, Councillors & Scrabblers, ammo
for Radical & Stately mouths, chuckled at in cartoons
of Ewen Me. English boxed on for 13 centuries since
Caedmon like fish'n chips love? cuppa tea love?
where's my CliffsNotes on The Odyssey, darling?
English's broadcast from the moon, is spoken
by our family, plus it's orbiting Saturn! Yet
Maori liberty is still recognized by Earth.

BRIAN TURNER

Fear

    I can tell you what fear is
and when it started.
    It's a policeman's little black book
and what goes down in it.

    Your father told you about it
and the consequences
    of misdemeanour, that crimp,
which became the book

    that grows under your skin,
watermarks of conscience throughout,
    contrition sharp as barley grass
in your socks, and like confessions

    hard to extract. 'Experience
is the best teacher,' Dad said,
    'and we're part of yours,'
Mum added, her eyes the colour of peat,

    except when joy dismissed
anguish whereupon they turned
    biscuit-brown, then lightened,
shone like acorns. You don't find

    peace there—at least I didn't,
and haven't—when you're downcast
    like a colt without shoes
standing in the fitful shade.

TIM UPPERTON

The starlings

Anger sang in that house until the scrim walls thrummed.
The clamour rang the window panes, dizzying up
　　chimneys.
Get on, get on, the wide rooms cried, until it seemed our
　　unease
as we passed on the stairs or chewed our meals in dimmed

light were all an attending to that voice. And so we got on,
and to muffle that sound we gibbed and plastered, built
shelves for all our good books. What we sometimes felt
is hard to say. We replaced what we thought was rotten.

I remember the starlings, the pair that returned to that gap
above the purple hydrangeas, between weatherboard and
　　eaves.
The same birds, we thought, not knowing how long a
　　starling lives.
For twenty years they came and went, flit and pause and up

into that hidden place. A dry rustle at night, fidgeting,
　　calling,
a murmuration: bird business. The vastness and splendour
of their piecemeal activity, their lives' long labour,
we discovered at last; blinking, in the murk of the ceiling,

at that whole cavernous space filled, stuffed like a haybarn.
It was like gold, except it was more like shit and straw,
jumbled with their own young, dead, desiccated, sinew
and bone, fledgling and newborn. Starlings only learn

a little thing, made big from not knowing when to leave off:
gone past all need except need, enough never enough.

LOUISE WALLACE

The Poi Girls

Kahu, Mere, and Faith
stand on the grass
by the corner.
They lean
on the fence and watch you
walk past—
spinning, twirling their poi.
Pou
Pou
Pou
The Poi Girls
say with their poi,
with each hard slap
of their poi.

On your way home
they're in the same spot,
Kahu, Mere, and Faith.
Their older brothers and cousins
are fixing the car, out
on Mere's lawn.
The boys stop as you
walk by.
They lean their hands
on the car's sides and look out
from under the hood.
What
you
want?
The Poi Girls
say with their poi.

You're walking
down the dip
but you have left
your shoes at school.
The yellow seeds
stick to your feet,
and when you get up
the other side, The Poi Girls
are looking
at you.
Om
Om
Om–mee
The Poi Girls
say with their poi.
Piss off,
you tell them,
leave me alone.
You don't need
their crap as well.

You stuff Pak 'n Save bags
into white plastic
and tie
them up with string.
You walk past the corner
twirling and spinning,
Hey
you!
Bumheads!
you say with your Pak 'n Save poi.
The Poi Girls chase you
down the street
but you are too little and fast
for them,
especially for Faith, the fat one,
the one with the lighter skin.

One day in the cloakroom
it's just you and Thomas
and he tells you
you have beautiful eyes—
green *and* brown,
just like his girlfriend, Jade's.
The Poi Girls burst in, twirling.
You
kissed
Thomas!
The Poi Girls
say with their poi,
your cheeks
pounding flush.

Your sister tells you
to run through the mud
and you say you will
and that you don't even care.
So you run
and halfway you sink
to your waist
and down the dirt road
come The Poi Girls, slowing
to a stop.
Ha!
You
egg
The Poi Girls
say with their poi
and leave
with your sister
in tow, twirling.

It's sunny but cold
that morning, on the way
to school.
Mere's front lawn

is filled with cars,
and there are people in suits
and old koros with sticks
and The Poi Girls stand
out the front.
Mere doesn't
look at you today,
so Kahu and Faith
glare twice as hard for her.
The Poi Girls' poi
hang still
from their hands
and today
say nothing at all.

IAN WEDDE

To Death

Death takes them all, that's why
We never see it. Death's never in
The picture. But everything we see, we see
Because death has. Death took the pictures.
Death looked at Chloe whom the poet

Begged not to run to her mother. Chloe
Ran into the oblivious arms of death.
Quintilius lies in the sleep that goes on
Without ever ending, and the music has faded away
That could have restored blood to the veins of the shade

Death saw. Lydia no longer
Wakes up to hear the sound of gravel thrown
Against her shuttered windows in the night.
Death pictured what lay behind the shutters
And Lydia grew old on the journey between

Her chamber and the dark street where death waited.
O passerby, do not refuse a few
Handfuls of sand to cover up the corpse
Of Archytas. It may be you who needs these rites
Some day, when death has viewed you as he did Archytas,

Who counted all the uncountable grains of sand
On the lonely beach. Death pictured my mother
And my father on the Picton foreshore, cheek by cheek
Under Gemini, twin sons unborn, tinkle
Of jazz from the ferryboat. And death looked at their sons.

SONJA YELICH

and-yellow

you realise there is no hope
left for teachers when in the
school newsletter it says
we welcome nichola poor
& look forward to working her.
you want there to be no more bell.
you begin to wish for pills for
your children instead of
lunch from a plastic décor box.
you wonder why their paintings
contain less & less
you begin to sound things out
stretching the oh's—
vowels start to look like
phone numbers
3 o'clock looks like a wedge of cake
you are rushing to finish
oh there you are tui
by dinah hawken
& then you hear
ella say:
and-yellow and-yellow and jello
angelo.
& he is
our number 4.

ASHLEIGH YOUNG

Certain Trees

One tree pretends to throw things
and the wind goes sprinting, then skids, turns—
ha! sucked in again, old wind!

One tree chooses to be apart,
like a door halfway up a wall.
My window groans with the weight

of trees
staking their territory. Humpbacked trees,
shipwrecks of trees

with piano keys inside
like the *Titanic*. Certain trees sway
holding lighted leaves up

as a voice sings out of a man
inside my neighbour's radio
why you on your own tonight?
The ones you shun always come back

to sing at you.
Certain trees reach for a woman
who is handing washing to the wind, a shirt

by the arms, pants by the waist, socks
by the feet;
        handing over parts of the body has never
        been so easy.

The wind sprints past the window again
        it gets dark quickly
and certain trees reach for me.

NOTES AND BIOGRAPHIES

FLEUR ADCOCK (2010)

Fleur Adcock was born in New Zealand but has lived in England since 1963. Her previous collections of poetry, now out of print, have been replaced by *Poems 1960–2000* (Bloodaxe 2000), and a new collection, *Dragon Talk*, appeared in May 2010. She has also published translations of Romanian and medieval Latin poetry, and edited several anthologies. In 2006 she was awarded the Queen's Gold Medal for Poetry.

Adcock comments: 'The following extract is from my journal, 20 November 2009: "I sat up in bed in the early hours of this morning and wrote an instant stream-of-consciousness poem called 'Having Sex with the Dead'. When I had finished the first 15 lines, I got up and went downstairs for a slice of toast and some hot milk, over which I wrote three lines more. (I was well aware that if I'd interrupted the flow of nocturnal dictation by getting up earlier it would have vanished). And that's it, more or less: I can't think of anything apart from the odd word that I want to change. It's such an odd production in any case that it would be difficult to judge it in the reasonable light of day." That afternoon I added: "But now, thinking about it, I realise that it has a lot in common with my other middle-of-the-night poem, 'Over the Edge', which really was based on a dream, not just surfacing thoughts from the deeps. However, as they were both sent from the subconscious I suppose it's not surprising that both feature water and dead people. I guess that's what we have down there."'

JOHANNA AITCHISON (2007)

Johanna Aitchison was born in the Bay of Islands in 1972. She left to attend Otago University, where she completed a Bachelor of Laws and was admitted to the Bar as a Barrister and Solicitor of the High Court of New Zealand. After graduation she worked as a solicitor at a Dunedin law firm, leaving in 1997 to do an MA in Creative Writing via Bill Manhire's pilot Master's programme at Victoria University of Wellington.

'Miss Red in Japan' comes from her second volume of poems, *a long girl ago* (VUP), which was a finalist in the poetry section of the 2008 Montana New Zealand Book Awards. She was the winner of the New Zealand Poetry Society competition in 2010, and her poems can be seen in *Big Weather: Poems of Wellington*, as well as online in *Turbine* and *Best New Zealand Poems 2008*. Johanna's third volume of poems, *Miss Dust Collection*, will appear in 2012.

She lives in Palmerston North with her partner and son and teaches creative writing at Massey University.

Aitchison comments: '"Miss Red in Japan" was written to express the sharp intensity of experience I encountered living for three years in Hokkaido, Japan. The inhospitable winters of Hokkaido—lasting five months and requiring lashings of snow shovelling—were just the trick for keeping the 122 million people in Honshu and Kyushu from seeping north.

'Miss Red in the poem created an imaginary family out of Moritz sticks, yellow plastic hard hats, frying pans. She found refuge from the bowing and the fierce buzz of staring eyes in the English films she rented from the local video store. She leached joy from the smallest of things—roadside vending machines filled with HOPE, LARK, Lucky Strike cigarettes, snow flying in sideways, and the crows, crows everywhere.'

MICHELE AMAS (2005)

Michele Amas was born in Dunedin in 1961. She has a degree in Performing Arts from Toi Whakaari New Zealand Drama School and has spent most of her working life acting and directing for stage and television. Her short film 'Redial' which she wrote and directed was selected for competition in the 2002 Venice Film Festival. She has an MA in Creative Writing from Victoria University and was the Adam Prize winner in 2005. Her first book of poetry, *After the Dance*, was published by Victoria University Press in 2006 and was a finalist in the Montana first Book Awards and the Prize in Modern Letters in 2007.

She shifts between acting and writing but maintains that acting and writing poetry employ the same observational skills, in one process you create more layers to flesh out the work and in the other you reduce the layers to an essence, they are both translations of form.

Amas comments: '"Daughter" was written out of a desperation to contain a myriad of emotions that living with a teenager forces you to experience daily. In this poem I have attempted to describe the shifting emotional landscape that a mother and child stumble into, quite out of the blue, both unprepared and bewildered—full of blame and guilt, need and love.'

ANGELA ANDREWS (2005)

Angela Andrews was born in 1977, in Rotorua. After graduating from medical school, she spent several years living and working in provincial New Zealand before settling in Wellington where she completed an MA in Creative Writing at Victoria University. She currently lives in Christchurch with her husband and four small chldren. Her collection of poems *Echolocation* was published by Victoria University Press in 2007.

Andrews comments: 'It was my first Wellington winter and I was walking with my son, who was several months old at the time. I was cursing the fact I didn't own gloves when I came across this large group of people gathered outside a house, only a block or so from my own home. The women were wearing beautiful white saris. As I got closer, I realised it was a family funeral, and the poem is pretty much exactly as I experienced it.'

TUSIATA AVIA (2004)

Tusiata Avia was born in 1966 in Christchurch, of Samoan/ Palagi descent. Tusiata is a poet, performer and children's writer. Her solo stage show, *Wild Dogs Under My Skirt*, premiered in New Zealand in 2002 and has since toured in Austria, Germany, Hawai'i, Australia, Bali and Russia. Her first collection of poetry, also titled *Wild Dogs Under My Skirt*, was published in 2004 by VUP. Her latest book of poetry, *Bloodclot*, was published in 2009, also by VUP.

Tusiata completed an MA in Creative Writing at Victoria University in 2002. She held the Macmillan Brown Centre for Pacific Studies Artist in Residence at Canterbury University in 2005 and the Fulbright Pacific Writer in Residence at the University of Hawai'i the same year. She was the 2010 Ursula Bethell Writer in Residence at the University of Canterbury.

Avia comments: 'I've got to admit, I blanched just a little when I first learned that "Shower" was to appear in this anthology. The subject matter speaks for itself. Putting a poem like this out into the public space (particularly as the only poem representing one's work) is a little challenging. In 2002 I was reading Sharon Olds—I love the way she writes about the deeply intimate. I find when I really connect with a poet's work it often gives me access to a "place" I haven't been to before.'

STU BAGBY (2005)

Stu Bagby was born in Te Kopura 1947. He is semi-retired and lives on a five-acre block of land in Albany, Auckland. Previously published in Auckland University Press's *New Poets 2*, his first full collection of poems *As it was in the beginning*, published by Steele Roberts, included 'The boys' and was nominated in the *Sunday Star-Times* by Kevin Ireland as one of 2005's best books. Stu is also the editor of *A Good Handful: Great New Zealand Poems about Sex* (AUP) and *Just Another Fantastic Anthology: Auckland in Poetry* (Antediluvian Press). His most recent collection of his own poetry, *So goes the dance*, published by Steele Roberts, was released at the end of 2010.

Bagby comments: 'A light, fun poem, "The boys" came from borrowing some cattle to bring my overgrown paddocks down after I'd fenced them off. I became quite fond of the boys and spent many hours in their company. I like to end poetry readings with this poem and use the final two words to exit the stage.'

HINEMOANA BAKER (2010)

Hinemoana Baker is a writer, musician, sound enthusiast and creative writing tutor. She hails from Ngāti Raukawa, Ngāti Toa Rangatira, Te Āti Awa and Ngāi Tahu on her father's side, and her mother's ancestors are from England and Bavaria. Her first collection of poetry, *mātuhi | needle* (2004), was released in New Zealand and the United States. Her second, *kōiwi kōiwi | bone bone*, was launched in July 2010. She spent three months in Australia as 2009 Arts Queensland Poet in Residence, and the Fall semester of 2010 in the US, as one of 38 Writers in Residence at the University of Iowa's International Writing Programme.

Baker comments: 'This poem is a response to the events of 15 October 2007 in Taneatua, Ruatoki and around the country, which have come to be known as the State Terror Raids. As well as being shocked by the methods employed by armed police on that day, which terrorised many innocent people, I found myself questioning the ethical decisions a person would have to make in order to be involved in the 12-month surveillance campaign which led up to the raids. I was moved to write the poem because of these things, and also after watching *The Lives of Others*, a film whose plot unfolds around the practice of surveillance by agents of the Stasi in East Berlin in 1984.'

DAVID BEACH (2003)

David Beach was born in England in 1959 to New Zealand parents who returned (with him) to New Zealand when he was five. From 1986 to March 2002 he lived in Sydney, since then back in Wellington. His poems have been quite widely published in Australia, without editors overdoing it. Since returning to New Zealand he has had poems published in the New Zealand *Listener*, *Poetry New Zealand*, *JAAM*, and *Takahe*; published two books with Victoria University Press, *Abandoned Novel* (2006) and *The End of Atlantic City* (2008), and won the Prize in Modern Letters in 2008.

Beach comments: 'From time to time I have flown in a plane, mostly between Wellington and Sydney, but have never jumped out of one. "Parachute" is from a group of "attack sonnets", where the idea was to write something energy high, sensibility unobtrusive. Yeats' "Leda and the Swan" was a key poem. Banjo Paterson's "The Man from Snowy River" also opened the door to possibilities.'

PETER BLAND

Peter Bland was born in Yorkshire in 1934. He emigrated from the UK to New Zealand in 1954 and began work with the NZBC to establish some of New Zealand's first arts and social commentary programmes. He was a co-founder of Wellington's Downstage Theatre and its artistic director 1964–68. He was associated with the Wellington group of poets and a close friend of James K. Baxter, Louis Johnson and Alistair Campbell, and his first substantial collection of verse, *My Side of the Story*, was published in 1964.

From the early 70s, Peter divided his time between England and New Zealand and travelled widely as an international jobbing actor for stage and screen. In the 70s and 80s Peter appeared in numerous West End comedies, as a guest artist on many UK television programmes, and at the Bristol Old Vic, the Chichester Festival Theatre and The Palladium. He settled permanently in Auckland in 2009. A *Selected Poems* was published by Carcanet in the UK in 1998, and his most recent book is *Loss* (Steele Roberts 2010).

Bland comments: '"X-Ray" was written following a medical check-up, which included a full-body x-ray. Studying the picture of this other person I felt as if I'd been playing host to some secret self who had uncomplainingly supported me for years. I sensed both an intimate relationship and a design-structure that I shared with the whole of humanity. The poem sprang from the ambiguities and insight of these feelings. I was delighted to discover, following publication in the New Zealand *Listener*, that someone had pinned it to the hospital notice-board. It's rare for a poem to find such an appropriate place in the "real" world.'

JENNY BORNHOLDT (2008)

Jenny Bornholdt's most recent collection is *The Hill of Wool (Victoria University Press* 2011). *The Rocky Shore* (2008) won the NZ Post Book Award for Poetry. She has written eight other books of poems, including a selected poems: *Miss New Zealand* (1997). Jenny was the Te Mata Estate New Zealand Poet Laureate in 2005/2006.

Bornholdt comments: '"Fitter Turner" is one of six long poems in *The Rocky Shore*. The poems all deal with similar themes—death, loss, the garden, poetry—and there's a kind of conversation going on between them. When I wrote this one I'd been thinking about the words "fitter turner" for a long time. They seemed good words with which to describe a poet.'

AMY BROWN (2008)

Amy Brown's first collection is *The Propaganda Poster Girl* (Victoria University Press 2008). She is working on a PhD in creative writing at the University of Melbourne. Her thesis involves writing a modern epic poem—whatever that might be.

Brown comments: '"The Propaganda Poster Girl" is quite a literal title for a poem about the figure in a Vietnamese propaganda poster, which hung on the wall above my computer while I wrote the book. After a year of writing mainly from my own point of view and about myself, looking up and seeing this surrogate subject was a relief. I think the poem became so long because I was enjoying writing it.'

JAMES BROWN (2006)

James Brown's four poetry collections are published by Victoria University Press. 'University Open Day' comes from *The Year of the Bicycle* (2006). James has been a finalist in the Montana New Zealand Book Awards three times. He is the author behind the informative booklet *Instructions for Poetry Readings* (Braunias University Press), and, in 2005, edited *The Nature of Things: Poems from the New Zealand Landscape* (Craig Potton Publishing). In 2010, a selection of new poems appeared in *Pocket Money / Against Gravity* as part of the Duets series—duetsbooks. wordpress.com—which pairs New Zealand and US poets.

Brown comments: 'I worked particularly hard on three aspects of this poem: the voice, the narrative and the form. The speaker is a school-leaver, so their voice couldn't quite be that of an adult, but anything too teenage would have been wrong, too. The nature of the voice naturally placed restrictions on the poem's language, reducing the scope for dazzling linguistic displays and, in so doing, placing extra pressure on the narrative as another way of engaging the reader. Like *The Year of the Bicycle* as a whole and many of its poems individually, 'University Open Day' is a journey. By the poem's end the speaker knows a little more about the world than they did at the beginning. Four-line stanzas are the form I use most in *The Year of the Bicycle*—especially in sections one and two where the younger protagonists require more structure. (In

section three, lists predominate, and, by section four, stanza-less
free verse has really kicked in). In 'University Open Day' the form
works like a series of rooms, through which the speaker and reader
move, pausing just long enough in some to sample the various
offerings. The offerings themselves are partly made up and partly
based on experience.'

ALAN BRUNTON (2001)

Alan Brunton was born in Christchurch in 1946 and died suddenly
in Amsterdam on June 27, 2002. He sent *Best New Zealand Poems*
the following biographical note on March 28 of that year:

'Alan Brunton has published nine books of poetry including:
Ecstasy, as well as compact disk: *33 perfumes of pleasure* (Free
Word Band 1997). Co-editor with Murray Edmond and Michele
Leggott of *Big Smoke: New Zealand Poems 1960–1975* (Auckland
UP 2000). Co-founder with Sally Rodwell of the experimental
theatre troupe Red Mole (ongoing since 1974) based in Wellington
since 1988 and previously in New York, New Mexico, London
and Amsterdam. Most recent theatre script: *Comrade Savage*
(Bumper 2000); most recent video production: *Crazy Voyage* (Red
Mole 2001). Has recently appeared at international festivals in
Colombia (2000), Denmark (2001) and Norway (2002), but not
yet in his own country.'

Brunton comments: '"Movie" is a death-trip; following the cortege
away from his father's funeral, a man gets lost, the journey fades
into an earlier one through the mountains of Portugal. Everything
falls apart, the man is left at his table with fragments of poems,
talking to someone who is not there. This poem provides part of
the text for the poem-video *Heaven's Cloudy Smile* and appears
also in *Ecstasy* (both available from Bumper Books, PO Box 7356,
Wellington South).'

RACHEL BUSH (2002)

Rachel Bush was born in Christchurch on Boxing Day 1941. She
grew up in Hawera on the west coast of the North Island. As a
young woman she wrote short stories, but she became increasingly

interested in writing poetry. Her two collections of poetry, *The Hungry Woman* (1997) and *The Unfortunate Singer* (2002) are both published by Victoria University Press. She has also appeared in Faber's *Introduction 3* as well as in anthologies and journals such as *Sport, Landfall,* and the *Listener.* Until 2003 she was a teacher of English at a secondary school in Nelson.

Bush comments: 'In the summer of 2002 a friend stayed with me. I'd first met her in 1950, but I hadn't seen her since 1964. We lost touch soon after that and now she lives in St Petersburg. We talked about Hawera, about growing up in this small rural town close to a beautiful mountain, and how desperate we were to move away from it. And we talked about our families, especially our mothers, how we loved them and took them for granted. It was her mother who knew how to make bread brooches and turn old gramophone records into vases.

   'People often say that in New Zealand in the 1950s women were preoccupied with housework and did nothing except care for their families and husbands. If they'd been young today, of course these women would have had longer careers in full time paid work and many of them would have had more formal education. Would they have been wiser or happier if they'd had these opportunities? I'm not sure. I do know they were distinct and strong and creative. When my friend went back to St Petersburg, I went on thinking about the mothers I'd known when I was at school. I don't think I set out to write a poem to celebrate their individuality, but this is what happened. I hope some of their particular ways of being human are clear in this poem. I like seeing their names in a poem. I miss these women. I'm glad I knew them once.'

KATE CAMP (2010)

Kate Camp is the author of four collections of poetry, all from Victoria University Press: *Unfamiliar Legends of the Stars* (1998), *Realia* (2001), *Beauty Sleep* (2005) and *The Mirror of Simple Annihilated Souls* (2010) where 'Mute song' first appeared.

Camp comments: 'This poem was inspired by a news story about a black swan in Germany which appeared to have fallen in love with an enormous plastic paddle boat in the shape of a white swan.

   'I wrote it after hearing the Canadian poet Christian Bök speak in Wellington. Bök's work, with its crazy ambition and gigantic scope, reminded me that poetry need not be limited to the possible, the real or the confessional; territories in which I had previously spent a lot—maybe too much—time.

'As well as this poem in the voice of a swan, my 2010 collection *The Mirror of Simple Annihilated Souls* includes poems written from the perspective of a donor kidney, a man with a sixty-year-long bout of hiccups, a one-armed Austrian pianist, and the white whale Moby-Dick.

'I think exposure to Bök's expansive poetic ego gave me license to explore this wider range of avatars, so I am happy that "Mute song" has now been published in his hometown of Toronto, in the literary journal *Brick*.'

ALISTAIR TE ARIKI CAMPBELL (2007)

Alistair Te Ariki Campbell (1925–2009) was a Penrhyn Islander who spent most of his life in New Zealand, which made him bi–cultural, existing somewhat uneasily in both the Polynesian and Pakeha worlds. He published drama, four novels, and many collections of verse, including *Just Poetry*, (HeadworX 2007) in which 'Tidal' appeared, and a joint collection of love poems, with his wife Meg Campbell, *It's Love Isn't It?* (HeadworX 2008). He won major poetry awards, including the Prime Minister's Award for Literary Achievement in Poetry in 2005.

Campbell comments: '"Tidal" was written on 1 June 2007 in the sad knowledge that my beloved wife Meg hadn't long to live. It was my last poem for her, and it is still the last poem I have written. "Alistair and I," she once wrote, "are both water signs, and come and go with the tide." Meg died on 17 November 2007.'

GORDON CHALLIS (2003)

Gordon Challis was born in 1932 in a family of Welsh origin who had, by then, moved to southern England. He emigrated to New Zealand in 1954 and trained in psychology and social work, later working in these two occupations—at hospitals and health centres—until retiring in 1988. He and his wife, Penny, now live in Nelson.

Challis comments: 'The setting for "Walking an imaginary dog" is the north coast of New South Wales where many caravan parks are sited on the wide estuaries. These parks are often run by the local shire councils who generally have a "no cats or dogs" policy. You can, however, have a caged bird.'

GEOFF COCHRANE (2005)

Geoff Cochrane lives in Wellington and sleeps poorly. In 2009 he was awarded the Janet Frame Prize for Poetry. His most recent book of verse is *The Worm in the Tequila* (Victoria University Press 2010).

Cochrane comments: 'My younger brother Stephen has for me much of the glamour of an older one. He remains lean and brown and good-looking, and still has a tendency to blush—when asking questions of bus-drivers or waitresses, for instance.'

GLENN COLQUHOUN (2002)

Glenn Colquhoun is a poet and children's writer. His first collection *The art of walking upright* won the Jessie Mackay Best First Book of Poetry Award at the 2000 Montana Book Awards. *Playing God*, his third collection, won the poetry section of the same awards in 2003 as well as the Readers' Choice Award that year. 'To a woman who fainted . . .' was published as part of that collection. He has also written four children's books and published an essay with Four Winds Press entitled *Jumping Ship*. In 2004 he was awarded the Prize in Modern Letters. He recently returned from a Fulbright scholarship to Harvard University where he was working on a collection of medical essays. He works as a GP on the Kapiti Coast.

About his poem, Colquhoun comments: 'It is based on an experience I had a few years ago at the Dans Palais during a Writers and Readers week in Wellington. An elderly woman fainted at the back of the tent during a poetry reading I had taken part in and I was beckoned from the front of the venue to help her. I found her pale and frail but she soon felt better lying flat and chatting while we waited for an ambulance. The trick, as most doctors will tell you, is to make people think everything is under control. This also seems true of poetry. The poem arose as a sort of quid pro quo for the situation. I guess that is why I adopted the mock serious tone. It was a way of taking any teasing I encountered afterwards seriously and considering the possible links between poetry and fainting as a conceit for a poem.

JENNIFER COMPTON (2009)

Jennifer Compton was born in Wellington in 1949 but now she is based in Melbourne. She is a poet and playwright who also writes prose. Her stage play *The Big Picture*, published by Currency Press, which premiered in Sydney and was also produced by Circa, was produced last year by the Perth Theatre Company. Her book of poetry, *Barefoot*, came out with Picaro Press in 2010 and her stage play *The Third Age* was shortlisted for the Adam New Zealand Play Award in 2011. She was Writer in Residence at the Randell Cottage in 2008, and Visiting Literary Artist at Massey University in 2010. Her poetry manuscript *This City* won the Kathleen Grattan Award and will be published by Otago University Press in July 2011. 'The Threepenny Kowhai Stamp Brooch' was first published in Quadrant.

Compton comments: 'It had been many years since I had spent time in my home town when I set up residence for six months at Randell Cottage in Wellington. And so much had changed. My friend Pam, who lives in Matamata, came to visit me, and gave me a brooch from the Te Papa gift shop which was a threepenny stamp, mounted in a metal frame, from back in the days when it was the usual postage for a letter. At least I think it was. I know I saw so many of them about that I think it must have been. It's a sprig of kowhai, with its beautiful yellow blossom, on a dark green background. Of course, pounds, shillings and pence have gone the way of so many other things. But there were wonderful new things that I noticed. The waterfront development had encouraged the strollers, the runners, the bikers, the skateboarders. I had recently spent time in Italy and enjoyed their promenade, their 'passegiata' and it struck me that Wellington now had one of its own, with a local flavour. And now, of course, unlike back in the old days, everyone pronounced kowhai as it should be pronounced. I doubted that this poem could work on the page, because I couldn't reproduce the difference in pronounciation of kowhai. But I wrote it anyway, because I wanted to. I thought I might read it a couple of times at gigs. It just goes to show you shouldn't distrust the intuitive intelligence of the reader. And already I have written more words than the poem contains.'

MARY CRESSWELL (2005)

Mary Cresswell is from Los Angeles. She came to Wellington in 1970. She is co-author (with Mary-Jane Duffy, Mary Macpherson, and Kerry Hines) of *Millionaire's Shortbread*, illustrated by Brendan O'Brien and published by University of Otago Press in 2003, and author of *Nearest & Dearest* (2009) and *Trace Fossils* (2011), both published by Steele Roberts. She has always worked as a science editor. She also lives next to the sea: this particular closeness and the goofy vocabulary of research science both have had a major influence on her imagination and will doubtless continue to do so.

Cresswell comments: 'The poem "Golden Weather (Cook Strait)" was first published by Richard Reeve and Nick Ascroft in *Glottis* magazine. It's my downstream response to the cryptic priorities of 1970 New Zealand: worship of the outdoors, how to preserve aged relatives/family values, the mysterious hierarchy of ritual foods, the sacred dog . . . to the language: "packing a sad" "on the day"? . . . and above all, to the red-blooded Kiwi family, that noble and indissoluble unit, Doing the Right Thing On the Day even if it bloody well kills us—or leaves us up Cook Strait without a paddle.'

ALLEN CURNOW (2001)

Allen Curnow was born in Timaru in 1911 and died in Auckland in September 2001. For more than 60 years, he was at the forefront of New Zealand poetry and literary debate. The anthologies he edited in 1945 and 1960 were seminal in shaping New Zealand's poetry canon. After training for the Anglican ministry (his father was a clergyman), Curnow turned to journalism instead and later lectured in English at Auckland University. His first collection, *Valley of Decision*, appeared in 1933. His last, *The Bells of Saint Babel's*, won the 2001 Montana New Zealand Book Award for Poetry.

Bill Manhire comments: '"When and Where" is a version of an untitled poem of 1829 by the Russian poet Alexander Pushkin (1799–1837). It is one of four translations made by Allen Curnow for Elaine Feinstein's *After Pushkin*, a book of translations, versions and responses to Pushkin by a range of contemporary poets, including Ted Hughes, Seamus Heaney, Eavan Boland, Carol Ann Duffy and Edwin Morgan. *After Pushkin* was published first by the Folio Society and then by Carcanet (Allen Curnow's UK publisher) to mark the 200th anniversary of Pushkin's birth. In New Zealand "When and Where" appeared in *The Bells of Saint Babel's* (Auckland University Press, 2001).

'The contributors approached by Elaine Feinstein were free to choose their own poems, and to arrive at their English texts as they wished. She did suggest, however, that translators might like to use as their starting point Walter Arndt's *Pushkin Threefold*, a compendium of Pushkin's verse which contained the Russian originals along with linear and metric translations. It is likely that the linear translation which Allen Curnow worked from is the Arndt text which begins, "Whether I wander along noisy streets/ Or step into a temple dense with people,/Or sit among fervescent youth,/I give myself over to my fancies." Arndt's metrical version went thus: "As down noisy streets I wander/Or walk into a crowded shrine,/Or sit with madcap youth, I ponder/Bemusing reveries of mine." The transformations effected by Curnow are dazzling.'

LYNN DAVIDSON (2009)

Lynn Davidson is the author of three collections of poetry, *How to live by the sea* (Victoria University Press 2009), *Tender* (Steele Roberts 2006) and *Mary Shelley's Window* (Pemmican Press 1999), and a novel, *Ghost Net* (Otago University Press 2003). Her poetry and short stories have appeared in *Sport, Landfall, Turbine* and *The Red Wheelbarrow*. She has a poem in the new edition of the poetry anthology *Big Weather: Poems of Wellington*, and in *Great Sporting Moments: The Best of Sport Magazine*. In 2003 she was awarded the Louis Johnson Writer's Bursary.

Davidson comments: 'Playing on the monkey bars at school is universal isn't it? You launch off, hand over hand, all light and rhythmical and fluid, and then the weight of your body slows you down. As a poet I am, of course, interested in rhythm and in risk.

I still look for the rhythm that will get me to the far side of the monkey bars. "He just doesn't swing" was the strongest criticism I ever heard my father make of a fellow muso. And he looked so sad when he said it, like being able to swing was the most important thing of all.'

FIONA FARRELL (2003)

Fiona Farrell was born in Oamaru, educated in Otago and Toronto, where she wrote her thesis on T.S. Eliot and poetic drama. Publications since include three collections of poetry, (*Cutting Out*, AUP 1987, *The Inhabited Initial*, AUP 1999, and *The Pop-Up Book of Invasions*, AUP 2007), two collections of short stories (*The Rock Garden*, AUP 1989, and *Light Readings*, Random 2001), and six novels (*The Skinny Louie Book*, Penguin 1992—winner of the New Zealand Book Award for Fiction 1993, *Six Clever Girls Who Became Famous Women*, Penguin 1996, *The Hopeful Traveller*, Random 2002, *Book Book*, Random 2004, *Mr Allbone's Ferrets*, Random 2007, and *Limestone*, Random 2009). Her work has appeared in various anthologies and she has been the recipient of several awards, including the 1995 Katherine Mansfield Fellowship to Menton, France. UK students have tangled with one of her poems, 'Charlotte O'Neil's Song', which featured in the GCSE syllabus. Charlotte also appears in Roger McGough's *Wicked Poems*.

Farrell comments: 'I wanted to write something dead plain about a meeting which moved me deeply. It's an "Our Trip" story, deliberately flat, in the tradition of those narratives we have been writing since primary school.

'The poem is "true", in the sense that we did indeed go to Takaka, where we met a young man sleeping on bracken, meditating in a cave. It seemed a noble and desperate thing to be doing: a traditional reaction by the young idealist in this beautiful muddle of a country.'

CLIFF FELL (2003)

Cliff Fell was born in London in 1955, to a New Zealand father and an English mother. In 1997 he moved to New Zealand, to Motueka, where he lives on a small farm and teaches in the School of Arts at NMIT in Nelson.

His poems have been published in New Zealand and the United Kingdom in magazines, chapbooks and anthologies, including *The New Exeter Book of Riddles* (Enitharmon, London, 1999), and have been broadcast on *Saturday Morning with Kim Hill* on National Radio.

In 2002 he graduated with an MA in Creative Writing at Victoria University and was the first poet to win the Adam Prize. His first collection, *The Adulterer's Bible,* was published in 2003, and his second, *Beauty of the Badlands*, in 2008, both by Victoria University Press.

Fell comments: '"Ophelia" was written in response to an exercise set by Bill Manhire—and as can happen with exercises, it ploughed open an unexpected furrow. The instruction was to write about "My pet", with the direction that the pet had to be imaginary. In my case, exercises usually stimulate immediate ideas, but this time I was completely stumped. It kept taking me back to Class 1 of Infant School, which wasn't somewhere I really wanted to go.

'Two days left until submitting and still not a dickey-bird. That afternoon, a murky April autumn day, we acquired a billy-goat. I watched in awe, and with a certain degree of admiration, as he ferociously served 14 of our 16 doe-goats in about ten minutes. It was then that it occurred to me that sex would be an unusual take on the "my pet" theme. But, goats? . . . no, somehow I thought not, wonderful companions though they can be.

'As it happens, I'd started reading *Jumping the Train Tracks with Angela* by Paul Durcan earlier that day, and later that evening I came across the fine and funny poem, I think it's called "The Giraffe", in which the poet ends up in bed with a fellow lover of giraffes. And that was it—it kicked me back to the late 1970s when I lived and travelled in Africa with a friend, the actor Guy Williams, now based in London.

'Guy had been born and brought up in Kenya, and as I reread the Durcan poem I recalled him telling me that during a particularly wild and lonely period of his teenage years, after he'd been expelled from school, he'd rescued and raised a baby baboon.

'I also remembered how fascinating it is to watch baboons in the wild—from a respectful distance. Out on the plains of East Africa their troops can number in the hundreds and take an hour or more to pass, during which time they display the full range of primate behaviours, not least the young adults' uninhibited onanism.

'But now, as the idea of a poem was beginning to take shape, all I could remember of Guy's baboon was that he'd called her Ophelia and that she'd once had him mistaken for the devil. I hadn't seen or spoken to Guy for eight years, but I had a phone number, and he answered. Needless to say, it was as if we'd last spoken two days before—and he was enthusiastic about the poem idea and immediately began to regale me with memories of his Ophelia . . .

'So, in some ways, the poem is a kind of found poem—there are lines, from the monkey's mouth, as it were, that are just as I scribbled them onto a scrap of paper, the phone clamped between my ear and shoulder. And when Guy stopped to comment on their relationship, to try and analyse it for me, and said her jealousy of friends and visitors was almost sexual in its intensity, I saw how easily I could take the poem into a deeper layer of "truth". I wrote most of the poem the next day, in about 45 minutes.

'And if my Ophelia has a quality of tenderness and emotion that is "almost human", as they say, it most likely comes from the nature of the other primates on this planet—and our relationship with them. In a recent copy of *New Internationalist* I came across this report by Abraham Odeke, of BBC Uganda, which illustrates what I mean:

Baboons protest road killing

A group of baboons by a busy highway in eastern Uganda became furious after a speeding lorry killed a female from their troop.

They surrounded her body in the middle of the road and held a 'sit-in', refusing to move for 30 minutes and blocking the highway completely, even when witnesses threw them food.

Last year a similar incident occurred when the baboons hurled sticks and stones at passing cars after a baby baboon was killed on the same road.'

New Internationalist, July 2003

SIA FIGIEL (2003)

Sia Figiel is. A mother. A daughter. A sister. An aunty. A cousin. A teacher. A painter. A novelist. A poet. But in her waking hours she works as the Literature and Language Arts Specialist for the Pacific Islands Centre for Educational Development in Pago Pago, American Samoa.

She won the Commonwealth Writer's Prize Best First Book

Award for the South East Asia-South Pacific region with her debut novel *where we once belonged*—'an extended poem', she says. She has written two other novels: *The Girl in the Moon Circle* and *They Who Do Not Grieve*, a prose poetry collection, *To A Young Artist in Contemplation*, and a CD recording of performance poems with Teresia Teaiwa—*TERENESIA*.

Sia Figiel's work has taken her to Paris, Berlin, Barcelona, New York, Honolulu, South America and she is the first Pacific Islander to read at the Shakespeare Globe Theatre, London. Her novels have been translated into Portugese, Turkish, Catalan, French, Spanish, German and Dutch.

Figiel comments: '"Songs of the fat brown woman" was inspired by one of my trips to London. I was in a shoe store, surrounded by all these African, Caribbean women. Of course we were all there because we had size 12 feet and we were looking for shoes. London (and most of the Western AND Eastern world for that matter) can be very unforgiving to women with big feet. Anyways, I spotted a size 13 and was about to dive for it when another brown hand grabbed it right before me. I looked up to confront the hand and she looked at me with a big smile and said: "Malo e lelei, tahine Hamoa." And that's how I met my Tongan friend Mavis!

'I was further inspired to write "Songs" after I met and had lunch with Grace Nichols at my then apartment in Berlin, a decade ago. Nichols is a former winner of the Commonwealth Prize for Poetry and is of course famous for writing the *Poems of the Fat Black Woman* BUT the difference is, she's a very skinny woman! I said to myself, someone with authority on fat has to be the one to write the songs of the fat brown woman! And the rest, of course, is history. Thank you.'

JOAN FLEMING (2008)

Joan Fleming's poetry has appeared in print in *Landfall, Sport*, the *Listener, Hue & Cry* and in the Duets chapbook series, which pairs New Zealand and American poets; as well as online in *Turbine, Snorkel, Blackmail Press* and *Lumière Reader*. She completed an MA in Creative Writing at Victoria in 2007, and won the Biggs Poetry Prize that year. Joan tutors writing for Massey University, keeps a garden, and practices Nichiren Buddhism. She lives, works, and writes between Wellington and Golden Bay.

Joan comments: '"Theory of light" is sort of a farewell poem. I wrote it after walking on the beach near my home in Golden Bay with a good friend. She had come to visit me before going back to America. This beach, I think I will claim it as the most beautiful place in the world. So much washes up and back, and the colours are unreal. On our walk, Andy was telling me about colour theory. She explained about wavelengths of light, and how the colours of objects aren't independent from the way our eyes perceive them.

'It made me think about how we only get back what we give out. It made me think about the things we carry with us, and what we leave behind. I don't fully understand any of this—colour, light, beginings, endings. But I hope this poem enacts a reaching for a way to understand. Re-reading it gives me a pain in my chest, in the best possible way.'

RHIAN GALLAGHER (2003)

Rhian Gallagher's first collection, *Salt Water Creek*, was published by Enitharmon Press (London) in 2003 and was shortlisted for the Forward Prize for First Collection. Gallagher returned to New Zealand in 2005, having lived in London for eighteen years. She received a Canterbury Community Historian award in 2007. *Feeling for Daylight: the Photographs of Jack Adamson* was published by the South Canterbury Museum 2010. In 2008 Gallagher received the Janet Frame Literary Trust Award. Auckland University Press is publishing her second collection of poetry, *Shift*, in 2011.

Gallagher comments: 'My father was *a man of few words*. He came out from Ireland in his twenties, worked on building hydro dams down south, then in the freezing works—hard manual labour. The physical act of burying him was my brothers' and my eulogy to him. There is a nod in the poem to the ritual involved in Catholic ceremony while at the same time wanting to break through the veneer when ritual turns into an empty vehicle. I am no longer a practising Catholic but it is impossible to escape such an inheritance. In Ireland it is often the men of the family who do the burial, my joining in pushed a little at the traditional male-only role. The physicality of the poem is important—I attempted to integrate this physicality into the writing itself.'

JOHN GALLAS (2009)

John Gallas was born in Wellington, brought up in Nelson and St Arnaud, but is at present in Coalville, Leicestershire. Eight collections published by Carcanet Press; the latest, *40 Lies*, in 2010. He works for the Leicestershire Behaviour Support Team in county schools. Writing at present a scientific version of *The Divine Comedy*.

Gallas comments: 'This tired poem is uncheerful only in the face of sublime beauty: heroic despair at approaching uselessness much occupies Mongolians. The poem was written after being weary, dazzled, transported and looking in the mirror, in that order, in Ulaan Baatar.'

PAULA GREEN (2004)

Paula Green lives in West Auckland with her partner, artist Michael Hight, and their two children. She is the author of five poetry collections published by Auckland University Press: *Cookhouse* (1997), *Chrome* (2000), *Crosswind* (2004), *Making Lists for Frances Hodgkins* (2007) and *Slip Stream* (2010). She has a PhD in Italian literature. Paula was Literary Fellow at the University of Auckland in 2005. In February 2005, she curated 'Poetry on the Pavement' as part of the Auckland City Council's 'Living Room' project. Paula has published two poetry collections for children, *Flamingo Bendalingo* (2006) and *Macaroni Moon* (2009). She is the poetry reviewer for the *New Zealand Herald* and has written and edited *99 Ways into New Zealand Poetry* with Harry Ricketts (Vintage 2010).

Paula comments: 'I once read a long list of associations that Ernest Hemingway made with rain that haunted me long after I had shut the book. A big fan of rain myself, I am quite happy to venture outside in the wet to walk in the bush, watch my girls ride horses, scramble over rocks, and ramble along the wild beach that is our closest beach.

'Placed on the first page, "Waitakere Rain" is a gateway into *Crosswind*, for in writing these poems I settled upon whatever had crossed my path and haunted me. I wrote this poem because as much as I love writing poetry, I love reading the poems of others. I love the way we can write our poetry on the sand (or the pavement, or the blank page) and upon each return find that it feels a little different. Above all, I love the notion that the world is plump with unwritten rain poems.

'I am also interested in the myriad crossings that make up our lives; the unexpected connections between places, people, memory, art, music. Sometimes, I test out my "crossings" in traditional poetic forms. In this poem, I crossed between my attachment to rain and that of Hemingway, between my poetry and his prose in a sonnet that has a hint of Petrarch, in rhyme more than meter.'

BERNADETTE HALL (2005)

Bernadette Hall's fifth collection of poems, *Settler Dreaming*, was shortlisted for the inaugural Tasmania Pacific Poetry Prize in 2003. *The Merino Princess: Selected Poems* was published by Victoria University Press in 2002. In December 2004, she went to Antarctica on an Arts Fellowship, with her friend and collaborator, the Dunedin artist, Kathryn Madill. Her Antarctic poems appear in *The Ponies* (VUP 2005). In 2006 she was Writer in Residence at Victoria University of Wellington and in 2007 she held the Rathcoola Residence in County Cork, Ireland. Her Irish poems appear in *The Lustre Jug* (VUP 2009), which was a finalist in the New Zealand Post Book Awards 2010.

Hall edited *like love poems*, a major selection of poems by her friend, the poet/painter Joanna Margaret Paul, published by Victoria University Press in 2006. She also completed a commission to write poems based on the Stations of the Cross sculpted by the Christchurch artist, Llew Summers, for the Cathedral of the Blessed Sacrament, Christchurch. She judged the 2005 Bell Gully National Schools Poetry Award and the 2006 Aoraki Poetry Award. In 2011 she is teaching in the MA programme at the International Institute of Modern Letters.

Hall comments: 'When I returned from Antarctica, everything seemed to have changed. It was as if I had brought Antarctica home with me to Amberley Beach. My eyes were drawn to patterns of ice and snow on the surface of the sea, in the clouds. As I walked along the track that runs through a pine plantation near our house, near a lagoon, I found myself thinking of the youthful explorers of the heroic age who had suffered in the "white warfare in the south", as Shackleton put it, only to find themselves embroiled in bloody fighting in Normandy. The immensity of Antarctica, its hazardous beauty, the way you are conscious of being "out of it" down there right at the end of the world, dependent on each other for survival, makes the thought of war, the tragedy and wastefulness of war, seem more terrible than ever.

'Iraq and Afghanistan were in my mind, the civil war in Ireland, the 19th-century land wars here at home. All wars merging into one. The Israelis, the Palestinians. There has only been one war in Antarctic territory, the Falklands war. Do you remember how belatedly we read of Argentinian boys, not much more than children, underequipped, underclothed, underfed, being stranded there? So much for the modern heroic.

'Terror is the feeling of the victim, of the trapped animal. "A war on terror" is a term that just doesn't make sense. There's enough terror inside me, inside all of us, I suspect, without adding to it. So that's perhaps where the poem is heading, into the dark plantation of our human fears.'

DINAH HAWKEN (2001)

Dinah Hawken was born in Hawera in 1943. She has lived in or near Wellington for over 40 years. For 20 years she worked as a student counsellor at Victoria University. Her six books of poetry, published by Victoria University Press, are *It Has No Sound and Is Blue*, which won the 1987 Commonwealth Poetry Prize for "Best First Time Published Poet", *Small Stories of Devotion* (1991), *Water, Leaves, Stones* (1995), *Oh There You Are Tui!: New and Selected Poems* (2001), *One Shapely Thing: Poems and Journals* (2006) and *The leaf-ride* (2011).

Of '365 X 30', she writes: 'It amused me to have this dream at the time of our 30th wedding anniversary. As you can see and hear, the poem is a very straightforward description of the dream up to the last two lines. The image in the second-to-last line was in my mind for months after I had had the dream and written the rest of the poem, but for some curious reason, which often happens, I wouldn't take it seriously. Then I realised, suddenly, that this spontaneous and concrete image was what I'd been looking for all along. Thirty years along.'

SAM HUNT (2008)

Sam Hunt was born in Castor Bay, Auckland, in 1946. He lived for a long time on and about the Cook Strait. He has published roughly fifteen books, including recently: *Doubtless: New and Selected Poems* (Craig Potton Publishing 2008), *Backroads* (Craig Potton Publishing 2009), *James K. Baxter: Poems Selected and Introduced by Sam Hunt* (Auckland University Press 2009) and *Chords* (Craig Potton Publishing 2011). An album with David Kilgour, *Falling Debris*, appeared in 2009. He now lives on the Arapaoa River of the Kaipara with his 13-year-old son.

ANNA JACKSON (2010)

Anna Jackson has published four collections with Auckland University Press, most recently *The Gas Leak* in 2006. *Thicket*, her fifth collection, comes out in July 2011. Anna lives in Island Bay, Wellington, and teaches in the English department at Victoria University.

Jackson comments: 'This was a throwaway poem I added at the last minute to a set of poems I was submitting to *Turbine*. I wrote it one day when fellow poet Erin Scudder and I were both chained to our computers and to make our day more amusing we set instant poetry challenges for each other. We would email each other a set of rules for writing a poem, and see how fast we could fire one back. The poem that became "Spring" just had to include three words Erin gave me. Probably "snow" was one of them, and I think another was "Montreal". I wrote the poem in less than three minutes and the only revision I made was to change "Montreal Avenue" to "diminishing avenues" which may have been a mistake. I have just found a copy of the original and it reads "you slink off down Quebec avenue / which is somewhere in Montreal", so the diminishing avenues are more of a revision than I remembered, and possibly even more of a mistake. "Quebec" must have been the other word I had to include to meet my obligations.'

LYNN JENNER (2008)

Until 2003, Lynn Jenner worked as an educational psychologist and counsellor, and read a lot. In 2004 and 2007 Lynn studied writing at Whitireia Polytechnic and in 2008 completed a Masters in Creative Writing at Victoria University. In 2008 her folio *Dear Sweet Harry*, a mixed genre work of poetry, prose, found text and visual images concerning the life and times of Harry Houdini, won the Adam Prize, and was published by Auckland University Press in 2010. 'Women's Business' appeared in that book without this title, and was known by the poem's first line.

Jenner comments: '"Women's Business" concerns some of love's nastier obligations. While researching First World War records for *Dear Sweet Harry* I became obsessed with why boys volunteered when they must have been afraid, and how their mothers let them go. Not why—how. Lots of people have written about this leaving and this letting go. Ernst Toller, a volunteer in the Kaiser's army, a leader in the German revolution of 1919, and a playwright, gives a young man's point of view:

> I died
> Was reborn
> Died
> Was reborn
> I was my own mother—that's all that matters.
> Once in his life every man must cast adrift from everything,
> even from his mother; he must become his own mother.[1]

'If my poem and his were jigsaw pieces, I think some of the holes and lumps would match.'

ANDREW JOHNSTON (2007)

Andrew Johnston is a New Zealand poet who lives in Paris, where he works as a freelance editor. Until recently he also edited The Page, an online digest of the web's best writing about poetry. His latest book of poems, *Sol*, was published in 2007 by Victoria

1   Ernst Toller, *I Was a German; The Autobiography of a Revolutionary*, translated by Edward Crankshaw, Paragon House, New York, 1991. First published Querido Verlag, Amsterdam, 1934.

University Press and in the UK by Arc Publications in 2008. In 2007 he spent a year as Victoria University's J.D. Stout Fellow, working on a book about contemporary New Zealand poetry. He has also edited *Moonlight: New Zealand Poems on Death and Dying* (Random House New Zealand, 2008).

Johnston comments: '"The Sunflower" is woven from many strands. In 1991 I read John Ashbery's book-length poem "Flow Chart" and was struck by the double sestina embedded in it (pp. 186–193), which borrows its end-words (among them, "sunflower") from a poem by Swinburne. In January 1997, newly arrived in the depths of a London winter, I was bowled over by an exhibition of Anselm Kiefer's sunflower paintings. When my father died in 2004, my brother Peter suggested two passages from the King James Bible for the funeral service; their language stayed with me. I spent November 2005 at a writer's residence in the north of France. On a trip back to Paris one weekend, I had a revelation in the train: I could use the double-sestina structure, and even Ashbery's (and Swinburne's) end-words, plus bits of the King James psalms and Kiefer's sunflower image, to write the poem I needed to write about my father (there are echoes of many other sources in there, too). I went back to the Villa Mont-Noir and wrote "The Sunflower".'

ANNE KENNEDY (2005)

Anne Kennedy writes fiction and poetry. She has won several awards including the Montana New Zealand Poetry Award and the BNZ Katherine Mansfield Short Story Award. She has worked in film, including adapting Dorothy Porter's *The Monkey's Mask* for the screen. Anne has taught fiction and screenwriting at the University of Hawai'i at Manoa, and is a co-editor of the online literary journal *Trout*. She lives in Auckland.

Kennedy comments: '"Die die, live live" is part of a narrative sequence about a young woman giant called Moss (*The Time of the Giants*), which is why the poem develops a bit of "story" towards the end.

'New Zealanders will recognize the title as a loose translation of the haka, "Ka mate, ka mate, ka ora, ka ora" ("I die, I die, I live, I live") composed by the leader Te Rauparaha in the early 19th century. These words begin the most well-known poem in

New Zealand. "Ka mate, ka mate" has long been commandeered by the All Blacks both to inspire themselves and to psychologically trample underfoot their opponents before play.

'Much of "Die die, live live" could be taken down in note-form in almost any New Zealand living room during a test match. I'd like to thank my husband Robert and his friends for handing me the language of rugby-watching on a plate, year after year.'

MICHELE LEGGOTT (2009)

Michele Leggott's sixth collection of poems, *Mirabile Dictu*, was published in 2009 by Auckland University Press, together with an audio CD of selected poems, *Michele Leggott / The Laureate Series*, from Braeburn and Jayrem. Michele continues to coordinate the New Zealand Electronic Poetry Centre (**nzepc**) at the University of Auckland and was the Inaugural New Zealand Poet Laureate 2008–09.

Leggott comments: '"nice feijoas" is a sign that appears each year in the neighbourhood, chalked on a blackboard near a table with bags of fruit and an icecream container for the money. It's a sign of late summer, as the light begins to change and your old dog reaches a steep patch in her decline, which is not yet a goodbye. In fact, she made it through the *Mirabile Dictu* poems; her ghost is present in writing that came afterwards and points to the time when a guide dog might enter our lives.'

GRAHAM LINDSAY (2003)

Graham Lindsay was born in Wellington in 1952. He has published seven books of poems, the last being *Lazy Wind Poems* (Auckland University Press 2003). He edited and produced the literary magazine *Morepork* (Ridge-Pole 1979–80), and held the Ursula Bethell/Creative New Zealand Residency in Creative Writing at the University of Canterbury in Christchurch in 2004.

Lindsay comments: 'It's a lullaby. I found caring for a baby, an infant, required such considerable attentiveness that the attention was rewarded with observations. "Arepa Omeka" is the Maori transliteration of Alpha and Omega, the beginning and the end.'

ANNA LIVESEY (2003)

Anna Livesey is a poet and policy analyst. Her second book, *The Moonmen*, was published by Victoria University Press in 2010.

Livesey comments: '"Shoeman in Love" is from my first book, *Good Luck* (Victoria University Press, 2003), written while I was a student at the International Institute of Modern Letters (IIML) in 2002. There is a small shoe-repair shop on the route between my then home in Mt Victoria and the IIML.'

CILLA MCQUEEN (2010)

Cilla McQueen was named New Zealand Poet Laureate in 2009 and in 2010 received a Prime Minister's Award for Literary Achievement. She has published over ten volumes, won the New Zealand Book Award for Poetry three times and received many international fellowships. She lives in Bluff.

McQueen comments: 'The Māori name of Bluff, a port in the south of the South Island, is Motupohue. Poets mentioned in "Ripples" are Joanna Paul (1945–2003) and Hone Tuwhare (1922–2008). The poem appears in *The Radio Room* (Otago University Press 2010), and was first published in the *NZSA Bulletin of New Zealand Studies* Vol 2.'

SELINA TUSITALA MARSH (2006)

Selina Tusitala Marsh is of Samoan, Tuvaluan, and English descent. She is a poet lecturing in the English Department at the University of Auckland. Her current obsession includes developing Pasifika Poetry Web, a sister site of the New Zealand Electronic Poetry Centre (nzepc). It is an archival site filled with poetry, interviews, biographical and critical information on poets of Pacific Island heritage in Aotearoa. Her poetry has appeared in the 2004 Montana New Zealand Book Award-winning anthology *Whetu Moana* and, most recently, in *Niu Voices: Contemporary Pacific Fiction 1*; a collection of short stories and poetry by Pacific writers (which she edited) as well as *Making Settler Colonial Space* (Palgrave Macmillan 2010) and *Mauri Ola* (Auckland University Press 2010); as well as on her sons' bedroom walls. Her collection of poetry, *Fast Talking PI*, was published by Auckland University Press in 2009, and won the Jessie Mackay Award for Best First Book of Poetry in the 2010 NZ Post Book Awards. She is working towards publishing her doctoral research as a book: *Ancient Banyans, Flying Foxes and White Ginger*, the first critical anthology of the first Pacific women poets to publish in English.

Nafanua: Ancient Samoan goddess of war, commonly myth-ologised, and renown for her battle prowess. She covered her breasts with coconuts and was believed to be a formidable male warrior until her womanhood was discovered.
Koko alaisa: a dish made from cooked rice, cocoa and sugar.
Faleuila: toilet.
Saka: boiled up dish (saka kalo is boiled taro).
Aiga: extended family.
Makeke fou: market place.
Kupe: money.
Kua back: villages 'at the back' or away from the more westernised (hence sophisticated) capital of Apia. Derogative in meaning.

KARLO MILA (2005)

Karlo Mila is a poet, writer, mother, columnist and academic of Tongan and Pakeha descent. She was born in Rotorua, grew up in Palmerston North, lived in Auckland for ten years and currently resides in Wellington. Karlo attended Massey University where she completed a BA in Social Anthropology and Sociology and a Masters in Social Work (Applied). She has recently finished her PhD in Sociology.

Karlo has had poems included in a range of anthologies and journals. Her poetry has been selected for *Best New Zealand Poems* three times. Karlo's first poetry collection *Dream Fish Floating* was published by Huia and won the 2005 Jessie Mackay Best First Book of Poetry at the Montana Book Awards. Her second book *A Well Written Body* was published by Huia in 2008. For this book, Karlo worked with visual artist Delicia Sampero creating images as well as poetry.

Karlo is now a Postdoctoral Fellow in the Social Psychiatry and Population Mental Health Research Unit at University of Otago, Wellington. Her postdoctoral research is focusing on what is healing for young Pacific people. She is examining narrative,

Polynesian myth, poetry, and metaphor in a therapeutic context. Karlo also writes a regular Op-Ed column in the *Dominion Post* called 'Pacific Current'. She lives in Newtown with her two sons.

Mila comments: 'This poem was inspired by a friend of mine, Teresa Brown and her circle of friends. They break all the "fobby" stereotypes of what Pacific people in this country are supposed to be like. They don't wear mumus or tupenu to their ankles. They are extremely well educated, ultra-urban, with sophisticated palates, good politics and basically they're downright fabulous. They're not afraid of who they are and they're not having cultural identity crises even though they don't fit the traditional Pacific "mould" . . .

'One of Teresa's friends, Victor Rodger, is a Pacific writer breaking down the stereotypes of who we Pacific people are supposed to be and what kind of box we are supposed to fit into to. I do have some concern about our art-forms sometimes, in that they (subconsciously or super-consciously) embellish the stereotypes that abound. Such as bunging a tapa pattern on a canvas or making references to hibiscus in a poem and somehow considering that to be "Pacific" . . .

'But essentially what this poem is also about—and what concerns me more—is the practice of deciding "what is not Pacific". I have come across so many cultural gatekeepers who try and control who we collectively are (e.g. Pacific academics, the highly visible community leaders and professionals etc). They often seem to have a very conservative and limited sense of "what" you must be and "how" you must be to be a "real" Tongan or Samoan etc. It is a bit of an "in" and "out" game, as subjective as those "what's hot" and "what's not" lists you see in magazines— except these are cultural scripts and tick-boxes.

'There is often such a disempowering sense of disapproval associated with "changing" and deviating from the imagined and "authentic" pathways of Polynesian identity and representation. Sadly for all us, these ideas of what constitutes authenticity can be far from actual Pacific realities in New Zealand. This poem was written as an in-your-face rant, basically . . . A bit of a backlash about these mean-spirited things we do to ourselves as a community.'

Fob: Fresh Off the Boat.

STEPHANIE DE MONTALK (2005)

Stephanie de Montalk was born in 1945. She lives in Wellington. A former nurse, documentary film maker, video censor and member of the New Zealand Film and Literature Board of Review, she came to writing late. Her four collections of poetry, published by Victoria University Press, are *Animals Indoors*, which won the Jessie Mackay Best First Book of Poetry at the 2001 Montana New Zealand Book Awards, *The Scientific Evidence of Dr Wang* (2003), *Cover Stories* (2005) and *Vivid Familiar* (2009).

She is the author of *Unquiet World: the Life of Count Geoffrey Potocki de Montalk* (2002) which was also published in Polish translation by Jagiellonian University Press (2003), and a novel, *The Fountain of Tears* (2006), after Alexander Pushkin's poema 'The Fountain at Bakhchisaray'. Her personal essay 'Pain' appears in *Sport* 33. She was the 2005 Victoria University Writer in Residence.

De Montalk comments: 'I wrote this poem from notes scribbled immediately after undergoing a bone scan. I had been somewhat apprehensive about the procedure—performed in a Department of Nuclear Medicine—in the way one often is, surrendering to the mercies of strangers and machines. In the event, I lay quite comfortably, albeit on full alert, in the scanner ("Hawkeye V4") listening to National Radio—beamed in from the control room— while the apparatus revolved and hummed in response to the radiologist who was entering his instructions into a computer: I lay comfortably, that is, until a preview of the news headlines announced Microsoft's discovery of a critical flaw in its software.'

EMMA NEALE (2002)

Emma Neale was born in 1969, and has lived in various New Zealand cities, as well as in California and England. She has a PhD from University College, London, and works in Dunedin as a freelance editor and writer. Random House NZ have published her five novels, the most recent of which is *Fosterling* (2011), and the collections of poems *Sleeve Notes* (1998) and *How to Make a Million* (2002). A third collection, *Spark*, was published by Steele Roberts in 2007. She edited the anthologies *Creative Juices: new writing* (Flamingo 2002) and *Swings and Roundabouts: Poems on*

204   *The Best of Best New Zealand Poems*

Parenthood (Random House 2008). In 2000 she was awarded the Todd/Creative New Zealand New Writer's Bursary, and in 2008 the NZSA Janet Frame Memorial Award for Literature.

Neale comments: '"Brooch", which is from my second book of poems, is perhaps best illuminated by a quotation from Emily Brontë's *Wuthering Heights*, which has always been eerily resonant for me (the memory and body a timpani, Brontë the quiet timpanist):

> I've dreamt in my life dreams that have stayed with me ever after, and changed my ideas; they've gone through and through me, like wine through water, and altered the colour of my mind.

'Of course dreams are notoriously punning phenomena. A brooch is "an ornamental fastening, consisting of a safety pin with the clasping part variously fastened and enriched" (from this the words "safety" and "clasping" leap out at me; the dream in the poem is one about vulnerability and loss). Yet the various meanings of the verb (to broach) are themselves synonymous with the actions of dreams: "to veer suddenly; to pierce or thrust through; to give publicity to, or begin discussion about". It seems to me that dreams often make us confront territory which the daily bustle diverts us from, or which we might deliberately try to skirt in our conscious lives. Dreams can behave like tough inner mentors that push us to our psychological limits.'

JAMES NORCLIFFE (2009)

James Norcliffe has published six collections of poetry, most recently *Rat Tickling* (Sudden Valley Press 2003), *Along Blueskin Road* (Canterbury University Press 2005), and *Villon in Millerton* (Auckland University Press 2007); and several novels for young people most recently *The Assassin of Gleam* (Hazard Press 2006) and *The Loblolly Boy* (Longacre 2009).

He was a longtime editor of *Takahe* magazine and is the poetry editor for the *Press*. With Alan Bunn and more recently Tessa Duder, he edits the annual *ReDraft* anthologies of writing by young people.

He has twice won the New Zealand Poetry Society's International Poetry competition, and has been shortlisted for the Montana New Zealand Book Award Poetry prize. With Bernadette Hall he was presented with a Press Literary Liaisons Honour Award for lasting contribution to literature in the South Island.

He has been awarded writing fellowships both in New Zealand and overseas, publishes poetry widely internationally and regularly reads at festivals and occasions throughout New Zealand and beyond.

Norcliffe comments: '"Yet another poem about a giraffe" is essentially a jeu d'esprit. I rather like the way rhyme can generate feeling, in this case that wobbly territory between pathos and bathos. The poem was prompted by a famous poem by the Russian Acmeist poet Nikolai Gumilev, for a period husband of Anna Akhmatova. Gumilev travelled to Africa a number of times and wrote many poems with African settings and about African creatures. Gumilev's "The Giraffe", perhaps written to cheer Akhmatova up, stresses the grace and wonder of the giraffe in its tropical home far from the "heavy mists" of Russia. I thought it would be fun to imagine the giraffe in Russia.'

GREGORY O'BRIEN (2005)

Gregory O'Brien is a Wellington-based writer and painter. Between 1997 and 2009 he was a curator at City Gallery Wellington, where he worked on exhibitions (with accompanying books) by Ralph Hotere, Rosalie Gascoigne, Laurence Aberhart, John Pule, Fiona Hall, Elizabeth Thomson and others. Recent projects include two major monographs, *Euan Macleod—the painter in the painting* (Piper Press, Sydney, 2010) and *A Micronaut in the Wide World; the imaginative life and times of Graham Percy* (Auckland University Press 2011). O'Brien's visual works often incorporate texts—his own poetry and that of others. In recent months, he has made a series of 12 etchings with John Pule (printed by Cicada Press, Sydney). He exhibits his work at Bowen Galleries, Wellington, and Jane Sanders Art Agent, Auckland.

PETER OLDS (2001)

Peter Olds was born in Christchurch in 1944 and now lives in Dunedin. His books include *Music Therapy* (Earl of Seacliff Art

Workshop 2001), *It Was a Tuesday Morning: Selected Poems 1972–2001* (Hazard Press 2004) and *Poetry Reading at Kaka Point* (Steele Roberts 2006). Earlier books include two from Caveman Press—*Beethoven's Guitar* (1980) and *Lady Moss Revived* (1972)—and *After Looking for Broadway* (1985) from One Eyed Press (Chris Moisa). He was Robert Burns Fellow at the University of Otago in 1978, and received a Janet Frame Literary Award in 2005. He has travelled widely around New Zealand, hitch-hiking and taking odd jobs. In his younger years, he spent time with James K. Baxter at Jerusalem on the Wanganui River.

'I made notes for "Disjointed" (in notebooks) during the late 80s,' he comments, 'while travelling around the North Island, shifting, broke, looking for something . . . Wellington Railway station was a favourite place for sleeping/shelter, and a meeting place for the 'down & out'. I'd been down & out myself on occasion, and sometimes when travelling around, half-broke, my path led back into it: sometimes just waiting for a train, a bus, something to open, to eat, or company . . . I've got notebooks full of this sort of writing. Another poem "Journey to the Far South" published in *Glottis 7* also comes from these notebooks.'

BOB ORR (2002)

Bob Orr was born in Hamilton in 1949 and now lives in Auckland. For many years he worked for the Auckland Harbour Board. His collections include *Blue Footpaths* (1971), *Poems for Moira* (1979), *Cargo* (1983), *Red Trees* (1985), *Breeze* (1991), *Valparaiso* (2002) and *Calypso* (2008). He has never shown much inclination to involve himself in literary journalism—or to write anything other than poems.

Orr comments: '"Eternity" is a poem from a section in my last book *Valparaiso* that deals with my childhood, or my recollection of it, on a Waikato farm during the 1950s and early 1960s. However in spite of its physical detail which could probably be verified by anyone driving that way (Huntly, not Eternity!) to me it works more on an imaginative level than a strictly autobiographical one.'

CHRIS ORSMAN (2002)

Chris Orsman was born in Lower Hutt in 1955 and now lives in Wellington. He has three main collections of poetry published, *Ornamental Gorse* (Victoria University Press 1994), *South* (Victoria University Press 1996 and Faber & Faber 1999) and *The Lakes of Mars* (Auckland University Press 2008), as well as chapbooks published by his own poetry label, Pemmican Press. In 1998, along with Bill Manhire and Nigel Brown, he was one of the inaugural Artists to Antarctica. His poems have been published in *Sport*, *Landfall*, *Takahe*, and *Printout*, and have been represented in a number of anthologies, including *Flora Poetica* (Chatto & Windus, London, 2002). He was the 2002 Writer in Residence at Victoria University of Wellington.

Orsman comments: 'The poem was commissioned by the Royal Society of New Zealand to commemorate the achievement of Maurice Wilkins, New Zealand-born pioneer of DNA discovery and 1962 Nobel Laureate. It was read at King's College, London, in December 2002, at a ceremony to mark the unveiling of an official portrait of Wilkins. Emily Perkins, expatriate novelist and short-story writer, read the poem on behalf of the author. The poem itself is an amalgam of biographical and scientific detail, beginning with a contemplation of a vanished birthplace and moving out into specific detail of Maurice Wilkins' scientific field (x-ray crystallography) and the extraordinary blue-print of the DNA molecule that he discovered. The poem finishes with a play of imagery around the original x-ray plate itself.'

VINCENT O'SULLIVAN (2002)

Vincent O'sullivan was born in Auckland in 1937 and now lives in Wellington, where he is a Professor Emeritus at Victoria University. No New Zealand writer has been more versatile. As well as his poetry, he has produced acclaimed novels, plays, short stories and literary criticism. With Margaret Scott, he has edited five volumes of Katherine Mansfield's letters. His biography of New Zealand novelist John Mulgan, *Long Journey to the Border*, was published by Penguin in 2003. *Further Convictions Pending: Poems 1998–2008* was published by Victoria University Press in 2009, and his latest collection, *The Movie May Be Slightly Different*, in 2011.

O'Sullivan comments: 'So many poems and stories are about being tossed out of the garden (usually Eden) that I was interested in one where people actually wanted to leave. And instead of it being a good place to be (the beginning of all) it was rather a grim place, a place where things ended. Perhaps the son and the father might be taken in different ways, but I didn't want them to be at odds as they are in the Eden story, but close and trusting before and after they pass the gates. A dead myth is good to leave behind; and winter of course is where so many myths die—at least for a while.'

VIVIENNE PLUMB (2005)

Vivienne Plumb writes poetry, prose and drama. She was born in the St George V Memorial Hospital for Mothers and Babies in Camperdown, Sydney, Australia (1955) to a New Zealand mother and an Australian father.

Her collection of short fiction, *The Wife Who Spoke Japanese In Her Sleep*, was awarded the Hubert Church Prose Award. Her first novel, *Secret City*, was published by Cape Catley Press in 2003.

Her poem 'The Tank' won first prize in the 1999 NZ Poetry Society annual competition. The poem 'Goldfish' appears in *Scarab*, a chapbook of twelve linked poems that are about the death of her son.

Vivienne has also been a recipient of the Bruce Mason Playwriting Award (NZ), the Buddle Findlay Sargeson Fellowship (NZ), a University of Iowa International Writing Residency (USA), and a Varuna Retreat Fellowship (Australia).

Plumb comments: 'I wrote this poem one night when I couldn't sleep. It's about the big ones: birth and death. It was written about my only son, Willie, who had Hodgkins disease (cancer of the lymph glands) and died at age 27 after a ten-year struggle against the disease. This poem was written at the beginning of his illness, when he was seventeen and undergoing his first course of chemotherapy.

'There is some interesting rhyming going on in "Goldfish". For me, the poem has a particular rhythm when I read it—a rhythm that changes three times. The dream in the poem was a dream my son really had, right down to the medical dictionary he was reading in the dream when he woke up.

'For some reason goldfish often appear in my writing—I did own two quite beautiful goldfish in a tank when I was a child, they often won prizes in the local pet competitions.'

CHRIS PRICE (2001)

Chris Price was awarded the 2002 NZSA Jessie Mackay Best First Book of Poetry Prize for *Husk*, in which the poem 'Rose and fell' appeared. In 2006 she contributed a verse essay, 'Are Angels OK?', to the science-art collaboration of the same name published by Victoria University Press. (An excerpt was subsequently selected for inclusion in *Best New Zealand Poems 06*.) She also published her second book, *Brief Lives*, a genre-defying work in the form of an eccentric biographical dictionary that was shortlisted for the Montana New Zealand Book Awards 2007 and chosen as one of Best Books of 2006 by the NZ *Listener*, Radio New Zealand National and LeafSalon. In 2008 she was Auckland University Writer in Residence at the Michael King Writers' Centre. *The Blind Singer*, a poetry collection exploring themes of music and perception, appeared in 2009.

Chris has worked as a book editor (for Century Hutchinson and Reed Publishing), and edited the literary journal *Landfall* for much of the 1990s. From 1992 to 2004 she was coordinator of New Zealand Post Writers and Readers Week for the New Zealand International Arts Festival. In 2004 she joined the staff of the International Institute of Modern Letters at Victoria University, and now co-convenes the Institute's MA in Creative Writing, as well as managing its outreach programmes. She is the 2011 New Zealand Post Mansfield Prize winner in Menton, France, and is published by Auckland University Press.

'While working on the final group of poems for my first book, I stumbled on the strategy of holding single words or phrases up to my ear like shells, and listening for the whisper of stories they might contain. "Rose and fell" was the title of a dance work by New Zealand choreographer Douglas Wright that I'd seen four years earlier. I don't recall what brought the title to mind again in 2001, but its two contrasting and perfectly balanced terms began to hint at a kind of fairy-tale narrative of good and evil. Some time in the preceding year, I'd listened to Seamus Heaney reading his translation of Beowulf, and elements of that epic (such as the figure of Grendel) also surface in the poem. The plant mentioned is rose-root, a herb which grows in rocky districts or on cliffs. Its root, when crushed or dried, gives off the scent of roses.'

KERRIN P. SHARPE (2008)

Kerrin P. Sharpe is a teacher of creative writing. She completed Bill Manhire's Original Composition class at Victoria University of Wellington in 1976. Over the last three years she has been published widely, including in *Best New Zealand Poems 08, 09* and *10*, *Turbine 07, 09* and *10*, *Snorkel, Bravado, Takahe*, NZ *Listener, Poetry NZ, Junctures, Sport* and the *Press*. In 2008 she was awarded the New Zealand Post Creative Writing Teacher's Award by the International Institute of Modern Letters. She was featured poet in *Takahe 69*.

Sharpe comments: 'A friend told me that when her mother died she heard her voice in a clock. I was fascinated by this and when I began writing the poem, I found myself back in St Mary of The Angels in Wellington. I could even hear the late Maxwell Fernie at the organ. It was very windy and I thought of the bell at St Gerard's Monastery (above Oriental Bay in Wellington). The St Gerard's bell became the prayer in the poem. Genya, the woman in the poem, was dying and held an apple, her link with creation and her Church. As she calls her children for the last time, their names become a glimpse into their lives without her.'

MARTY SMITH (2009)

Marty Smith was born in the 1950s. She grew up on a remote and wild hill country farm in north Wairarapa, cleared from the native bush by her great-grandfather in the 1800s.

She teaches at Taradale High School in Hawkes Bay. She has an MA in Creative Writing from Victoria University and is working on a series of poems which move sometimes in the racing world and sometimes in the war between her father and almost everything.

Smith comments: 'My father didn't speak to my grandmother for eighteen years, then he died first.'

ELIZABETH SMITHER (2006)

Elizabeth Smither was New Zealand's first woman Te Mata Estate Poet Laureate (2001–3), and received the Prime Minister's Award for Literary Achievement in Poetry in 2008. She has published numerous collections of poetry as well as novels and short stories. Her latest book is *The Commonplace Book: A Writer's Journey Through Quotations* (Auckland University Press 2011).

Smither comments: 'At the end of each day's work at Puke Ariki two librarians in their black uniforms plus two guards (armed with torches and walkie-talkies) would carry the day's takings from the adult and children's libraries, the reference room, to be deposited in the safe on the top floor. I always used to enjoy this moment: our heels ringing on the board floor, the two guards following behind, the little bags and the cash tin (with about enough takings inside to get us to Eketahuna). The safe (a small squat affair with a golden design on the door and formidable teeth which you had to make sure meshed) was in a room housing old uniforms and spare furniture. The guards waited while the bags and floats and cash box were stowed and the long thin safe key turned and left in its lock. (Someone could open the safe if they were locked in the room and count the takings).

'The night of the poem I was eavesdropping on the guards talking about Jupiter and noting the differences between male and female conversations—the male concentration on facts—the facts of Jupiter and the Earth were offered in the manner we had offered money to the safe. As we walked back, glimpsing the starry evening sky through the long windows, Jupiter seemed the perfect and hopeful end to the day.'

C.K. STEAD (2004)

C.K. Stead ONZ CBE FRSL is a leading figure in Commonwealth literature—novelist, poet, critic, teacher, and the author of many books. Christian Karlson (Karl) Stead was born in New Zealand in 1932. He lives in Auckland but spends a part of each year living and writing overseas. He is married with three children, one of whom, Charlotte Grimshaw, is also a writer. C.K. Stead received the Prime Minister's Award for Literary Achievement in 2009.

His *Collected Poems, 1951–2006* was published in 2008, and

South-West of Eden: A Memoir, 1932–1956 in 2010, both by Auckland University Press.

Stead comments: 'This is one of my 13-syllable triplet poems—a number I've written in recent years have found their way into that casual and yet quite demanding form. The poem comes from a story about Allen Curnow, on his way home after completing his training for the Anglican priesthood, finding he had lost his faith. I have fictionalised it, so he isn't named.'

RICHARD VON STURMER (2008)

Richard von Sturmer is a New Zealand writer and filmmaker. His books are: *We Xerox Your Zebras* (Modern House 1988), *A Network of Dissolving Threads* (Auckland University Press 1991), *Suchness: Zen Poetry and Prose* (HeadworX 2005), and *On the Eve of Never Departing* (Titus Books 2009).

As well as being a lyricist for several New Zealand bands, including Blam Blam Blam, he and his partner, Amala Wrightson, toured the country in the 1980s as the performing duo, The Humanimals. From 1993 to 2003 he lived and worked at the Rochester Zen Center, a Buddhist community in upstate New York. During that time his work appeared regularly in literary journals and anthologies.

von Sturmer comments: 'In the 1990s, living in upstate New York, I was separated from my library. A modest library in many respects, but one which I had created, willy-nilly, since my teenage years. One of the joys of relocating back to Auckland in 2004 was to be reunited with my collection of books. Since then many have remained unopened on their shelves, but once and a while I like to take down an old favourite and open its pages. One such volume is *The Collected French Writings of Jean Arp*, edited by Marcel Jean and translated by Joachim Neugroschel. Although Arp is better known for his sculpture and painting, he produced wonderfully imaginative poetry all his life. His surrealistic poems have a very pure quality, and when I happened to read through them once again last year, they triggered atavistic surrealist tendencies in my own writing. The result was "After Arp", which I produced in two quick bursts. Arp stated that "It was in dreams that I learned how to write, and it was only much later that I laboriously learned how to read." So it happened that "Mushrooms", the poem that launches the series, came from a dream I had about black mushrooms with long green hair. According to the Polish writer Stanislaw Lem, "A dream can only be where there is a reality to return to." In this spirit the series closes with "Captain Cook's Hat", which is a small outcrop of rock, visible from the shore of Vanuatu's volcanic island of Tanna. And yes, there is one small tree growing on the top and one on the side.'

ROBERT SULLIVAN (2007)

Robert Sullivan is of Maori (Ngā Puhi/Kai Tahu/Ngāti Raukawa) and Galway Irish descent. His poetry collections include *Voice Carried My Family* (AUP), *Shout Ha! to the Sky* (Salt, UK, 2010), *Cassino City of Martyrs / Città Martire* (Huia 2010). He co-edited *Whetu Moana: Contemporary Polynesian Poems in English* with Albert Wendt and Reina Whaitiri, while the follow-up volume *Mauri Ola* was published in 2010. He has recently read and lectured in New Delhi at the Chotro Indigenous Peoples Conference, UC Berkeley, UCLA, University of Hong Kong, Goethe University in Frankfurt, Universitats de les Illes Balears in Spain and the European Commonwealth Languages and Literatures Association triennial conference in Istanbul. He is Head of Creative Writing at Manukau Institute of Technology, having recently returned from the University of Hawai'i at Manoa where for a time he was Director of Creative Writing.

Sullivan comments: 'This poem comes from a section of my next book devoted to the recent controversy surrounding Maori customary use and local Maori ownership of the foreshore and seabed. A simple majority in Parliament removed these property rights built up by Maori tribes with coastal access over 800–1000 years. The main right removed was the one to advocate in Court for these ownership interests (where advocacy is the right to speak effectively, to argue within and not outside the acknowledged conventions of the legal system). The poem refers to Caedmon, English history, and European literature, in an attempt to draw Pakeha readers' attention to their own literary and customary heritage. One should not explain poetry though.

'In New Zealand currently there are few checks and balances on its one–house legislature since a simple majority, with the signature of the Governor General, might suspend or remove many privileges and rights of citizens without independent binding review. Luckily there was one extra check that the government could not suspend, via a United Nations Special Rapporteur who briefly embarrassed the current government by issuing a critical report in support of Maori.'

Hupe: mucous.
Wahangu: mute, quiet.

BRIAN TURNER (2009)

Brian Turner is one of New Zealand's more versatile writers whose work includes best-selling biographies of sporting 'greats' and numerous collections of poetry.

Turner won the Commonwealth Poetry Prize for his first volume *Ladders of Rain* and the New Zealand Book Award for Poetry for his collection *Beyond*. In 1994–5 he held the Arts Council Scholarship in Letters. He was Robert Burns Fellow at the University of Otago in 1984, Writer in Residence at the University of Canterbury in 1997, and in 2003–5 he was the Te Mata Estate New Zealand Poet Laureate.

His most recent books are the best-selling *Into the Wider World* (shortlisted for the 2009 Montana Book Awards), essays and poems which focus on his love of and concerns for the future of this country's natural environment, and the poetry collections *Just This*, which contains a substantial number of new poems set in Central Otago, and *Inside Outside*.

In 2009 he received the Prime Minister's Award for Literary Achievement in Poetry. Also in 2009, he was awarded the Lauris Edmond Memorial Award for his 'distinguished contribution to New Zealand Poetry'. In 2010 *Just This* won the New Zealand Post Book Award for Poetry.

Turner comments: 'When I think of my more dominant personal characteristics, the one that springs immediately to mind is fearfulness. I was, my parents often said, a "nervy kid". I still am nervy, lack confidence, don't have enough faith in my own abilities, and tend to fret about and dwell on my mistakes. I'm poor at what is frequently termed—and how I dislike the phrase—"moving on". I've never forgotten the first time I felt extremely fearful. As I say in the poem, it was when my father, jocularly, as I came to see later, threatened to report me to the local cop. At the time, I wouldn't have been more than four years of age. And for decades after I was inclined to be fearful of anyone in authority. I hated that because such fear drives deference, and don't the worst sods take advantage of that.

'The poem also alludes to another trait of mine that I dislike, self–flagellation, or an inclination to blame myself when things go awry. I've often been told I've been "too hard" on myself, and some have said that I'm a masochist. I disagree, nonetheless it's irksome to hear it.

'But there's more to the poem than that. In the end it works up to referring to something that was common to both my parents, and to me, and that is the extent to which our experiences swung back and forth from anguish to joy, and how difficult it is to banish the former and stay on a fairly even keel. As for the reference to "peace", I have this nagging feeling that it's something many people, and most poets, long for but seldom, if ever, find. Or if so, not for long.'

TIM UPPERTON (2009)

Tim Upperton's poetry and fiction are published or forthcoming in *AGNI* (US), *Bravado, Dreamcatcher* (UK), *Landfall, New Zealand Books*, New Zealand *Listener, North & South, Reconfigurations* (US), *Sport, Takahe, Turbine* and *Best New Zealand Poems*. He is a former poetry editor for *Bravado*, and tutors creative writing, travel writing and New Zealand literature at Massey University. His first poetry collection, *A House On Fire*, was published by Steele Roberts in 2009.

Tim Upperton comments: '"The starlings" was originally an informal epithalamion, a poem to commemorate the wedding of my sister, Katrina, and her husband, Steve. That version was, appropriately enough, a lot more celebratory than the final version you see here. The poem includes details my sister would remember, such as the immense starlings' nest in the ceiling of our family home. I kept revisiting and revising this poem following its first publication in the NZ Poetry Society's anthology *tiny gaps* (2006), and each time it got a little darker than before—notes of elegy seeped in. A last-minute change before my first book of poems,

A House on Fire, went to print was the addition of the word "murmuration"—a lovely old collective noun for starlings.'

LOUISE WALLACE (2009)

Louise Wallace's first collection of poetry, *Since June*, was released in December 2009 through Victoria University Press. Louise completed an MA in Creative Writing at the International Institute of Modern Letters in 2008, and her poems have previously appeared in a variety of literary journals including *Meanjin*, *Turbine* and *Sport*.

Wallace comments: '"The Poi Girls" is one of those rare poems that came to me almost fully-formed in the middle of the night. The rhythm was a big part of that. I scribbled it down then and there, and I wish this happened more often! I grew up in Gisborne, a place I love, and the essence of this poem comes from there. The poem is about childhood, curiosity and the nature of difference, but contains a certain menace too. I hoped to convey the weight and seriousness that events so often have when you experience them as a child.'

IAN WEDDE (2001)

Ian Wedde was born in Blenheim in 1946. He spent part of his childhood in East Pakistan (now Bangladesh) and England before returning to New Zealand at age 15. One of the most admired poets of his generation, he has also written novels, short stories and art criticism. In the mid-1980s he co-edited the ground-breaking *Penguin Book of New Zealand Verse* with Harvey McQueen. From 1994 to 2004, he was curator of art and visual culture at the Museum of New Zealand Te Papa Tongarewa. *The Commonplace Odes* (2001) marked his return to poetry after a hiatus of nearly a decade.

Wedde comments: 'Death is one of the themes in *The Commonplace Odes* which winds right through the book and is the main business of the final poem, "Carmen Saeculare". It is there (the theme) in formal ways, as a kind of address—the gravity of the funerary ode, sombre, and respectful of grief; and it is there (the theme of death) as a flipside of anarchic appetite, disrespectful of ordinariness which is not lived as though this life were your last. "To Death" has borrowed a number of personifications of death from the odes of Horace (Chloe, Quintillius, Lydia, Archytas, etc) and has threaded them on an idea carried over from the previous ode (mine not Horace's) which derives from my own long-dead father's lifelong habit of taking photographs. Because he took them, he was never in them. We don't see death, because he takes the pictures. Death pictures something, he frames it up, it's going to die. So get a life.'

SONJA YELICH (2002)

Sonja Yelich was born in Auckland in 1965. She is a first-generation New Zealander and lives with her partner and four children in Devonport, Auckland. Her work was published in 2002 by Auckland University Press in the *AUP New Poets* series which includes the writing of three emerging NZ poets. *Clung* (AUP 2004) won the 2005 NZSA Jessie Mackay Award for Best First Book of Poetry, and was followed by *get some* (AUP 2008).

Yelich comments: 'While the ideas in "and-yellow" are true, well sort of, they didn't actually happen in that order. In fact, they are bits of ideas taken from different days and put together to give a kind of "one take" sort of impression. I like doing that type of writing probably because I do that sort of thinking—here and here and then there. And that's probably got something to do with the fact that I've got four small kids who get around like loose bees—and into the poems.'

ASHLEIGH YOUNG (2009)

Ashleigh Young grew up in Te Kuiti and Wellington. Her poems and essays have appeared in *Booknotes, Turbine, Sport, Landfall*, and the *School Journal*. Ashleigh was the winner of the 2009 Landfall Essay Competition and the recipient of the 2009 Adam Prize in Creative Writing. She has worked as an editor at Learning Media and is currently an editor at the Aga Khan University in London.

Young comments: 'I wrote this poem when I was living on my own and listening to a lot of The Smiths—never a very healthy combination. Maybe Morrissey got into my bones and I got a bit miserable. I had the sense that I was shrinking and the world outside was growing and becoming more animated—especially the trees, these prickly, wonky, very anti-picture-book trees. The more time I spent alone in my little flat, the more perspective I lost, and those trees began to seem quite powerful. I suppose it was a bit like when you're a kid and convinced that aliens are hiding under your bed or behind the curtains. It makes no sense now, but it made perfect sense at the time. The line "Why you on your own tonight?" is from a Smiths song.'

All poems from *Best New Zealand Poems* over the last decade, plus individual editors' introductions and many useful links, can be accessed at

http://www.victoria.ac.nz/bestnzpoems

You can also find most of the poems in this book read by their authors at the same web address.

COPYRIGHT ACKNOWLEDGEMENTS

Gordon Challis, 'Walking an imaginary dog', from *The Other Side of the Brain* (Steele Roberts 2003), reprinted with permission of the poet and Steele Roberts.

Geoff Cochrane, 'Seven Unposted Postcards to My Brother', from *84 484* (Victoria University Press 2007), reprinted with permission of the poet.

Glenn Colquhoun, 'To a woman who fainted recently at a poetry reading', from *Playing God* (Steele Roberts 2002), reprinted with permission of the poet and Steele Roberts.

Jennifer Compton, 'The Threepenny Kowhai Stamp Brooch', from *This City* (University of Otago Press 2011) reprinted with permission of the poet.

Mary Cresswell, 'Golden Weather (Cook Strait)', from *Trace Fossils* (Steele Roberts 2011) reprinted with permission of the poet and Steele Roberts.

Allen Curnow, 'When and Where', from *The Bells of Saint Babel's* (Auckland University Press 2001), reprinted with permission of the estate of Allen Curnow and Auckland University Press.

Lynn Davidson, 'Before we all hung out in cafés', from *How to Live by the Sea* (Victoria University Press 2009), reprinted with permission of the poet.

Fiona Farrell, 'Our trip to Takaka', reprinted with permission of the poet.

Cliff Fell, 'Ophelia', from *The Adulterer's Bible* (Victoria University Press 2003), reprinted with permission of the poet.

Sia Figiel, 'Songs of the fat brown woman', reprinted with permission of the poet.

Joan Fleming, 'Theory of light', reprinted with permission of the poet.

Rhian Gallagher, 'Burial', from *Salt Water Creek* (Enitharmon 2003), reprinted with permission of the poet.

John Gallas, 'the Mongolian Women's Orchestra', reprinted with permission of the poet.

Paula Green, 'Waitakere Rain', from *Crosswind* (Auckland University Press 2004), reprinted with permission of the poet and Auckland University Press.

Bernadette Hall, 'The History of Europe', from *The Ponies* (Victoria University Press 2007), reprinted with permission of the poet.

Dinah Hawken, '365 x 30', from *Oh There You Are Tui!* (Victoria University Press 2001), reprinted with permission of the poet.

Sam Hunt, 'Lines for a New Year', from *Doubtless: New and Selected Poems* (Craig Potton Publishing, 2008), reprinted with permission of the poet and Craig Potton Publishing.

Anna Jackson, 'Spring', from *Thicket* (Auckland University Press 2011), reprinted with permission of the poet and Auckland University Press.

Lynn Jenner, 'Women's Business', from *Dear Sweet Harry* (Auckland University Press 2010), reprinted with permission of the poet and Auckland University Press.

Andrew Johnston, 'The Sunflower', from *Sol* (Victoria University Press 2007), reprinted with permission of the poet.

Anne Kennedy, 'Die die, live live', from *The Time of the Giants* (Auckland University Press 2005), reprinted with permission of the poet and Auckland University Press.

Michele Leggott, 'nice feijoas', from *Mirabile Dictu* (Auckland University Press 2009), reprinted with permission of the poet and Auckland University Press.

Graham Lindsay, 'big bed', from *Lazy Wind Poems* (Auckland University Press 2003), reprinted with permission of the poet and Auckland University Press.

Anna Livesey, 'Shoeman in Love', from *Good Luck* (Victoria University Press 2003), reprinted with permission of the poet.

Cilla McQueen, 'Ripples', from *The Radio Room* (University of Otago Press 2010) reprinted with permission of the poet and University of Otago Press.

Bill Manhire, 'The Next Thousand', from *Collected Poems* (Victoria University Press, 2001), reprinted with permission of the poet.

Selina Tusitala Marsh, 'Not Another Nafanua Poem', from *Fast Talking PI* (Auckland University Press 2009), reprinted with permission of the poet and Auckland University Press.

Karlo Mila, 'Sacred Pulu', from *Dream Fish Floating* (Huia 2005), reprinted with permission of the poet and Huia.

Stephanie de Montalk, 'Hawkeye V4', from *Cover Stories* (Victoria University Press 2005), reprinted with permission of the poet.

Emma Neale, 'Brooch', from *How to Make a Million* (Godwit 2002), reprinted with permission of the poet.

James Norcliffe, 'yet another poem about a giraffe', reprinted with permission of the poet.

Gregory O'Brien, 'Where I Went', from *Afternoon of An Evening Train* (Victoria University Press 2005), reprinted with permission of the poet.

Peter Olds, 'Disjointed on Wellington Railway Station', reprinted with permission of the poet.

Bob Orr, 'Eternity', from *Valparaiso* (Auckland University Press 2002), reprinted with permission of the poet and Auckland University Press.

Chris Orsman, 'Making Waves', from *The Lakes of Mars* (Auckland University Press 2008), reprinted with permission of the poet and Auckland University Press.

Vincent O'Sullivan, 'The Child in the Gardens: Winter', from *A Nice Morning for It, Adam* (Victoria University Press 2004), reprinted with permission of the poet.

Vivienne Plumb, 'Goldfish', from *Scarab: A Poetic Documentary* (Seraph Press 2005) reprinted with permission of the poet and Seraph Press.

Chris Price, 'Rose and fell', from *Husk* (Auckland University Press 2002), reprinted with permission of the poet and Auckland University Press.

Kerrin P. Sharpe, 'like rain the thunder', reprinted with permission of the poet.

Marty Smith, 'Hat', reprinted with permission of the poet.

Elizabeth Smither, 'Two security guards talking about Jupiter', from *A Year of Adverbs* (2007), reprinted with permission of the poet and Auckland University Press.

C.K. Stead, 'Without', from *Collected Poems, 1951–2006* (Auckland University Press 2008), reprinted with permission of the poet and Auckland University Press.

Richard von Sturmer, 'After Arp', reprinted with permission of the poet.

Robert Sullivan, 'After the UN Rapporteur Supported Maori Customary Rights', from *Shout Ha! to the Sky* (Salt 2010), reprinted with permission of the poet.

Brian Turner, 'Fear', from *Just This* (Victoria University Press 2009), reprinted with permission of the poet.

Tim Upperton, 'The starlings', from *A House on Fire* (Steele Roberts 2009), reprinted with permission of the poet and Steele Roberts.

Louise Wallace, 'The Poi Girls', from *Since June* (Victoria University Press 2009), reprinted with permission of the poet.

Ian Wedde, 'To Death', from *The Commoplace Odes* (Auckland University Press 2001), reprinted with permission of the poet and Auckland University Press.

Sonja Yelich, 'and-yellow', from *Clung* (Auckland University Press 2004), reprinted with permission of the poet and Auckland University Press.

Ashleigh Young, 'Certain Trees', reprinted with permission of the poet.